# AN ESSENTIAL GUIDE TO AGING WELL

This book is a refreshingly honest self-help guide to aging well. It encourages readers to dispel gloom or overcome denial around the subject of aging and offers advice in a realistic, non-prescriptive format.

Practical yet personable, chapters move through pertinent topics such as making the decision to retire and successfully navigating that transition; designing daily routines (your *practice*) and engaging in activities (your *projects*); connecting with others as relationships shift and evolve; and managing moods and emotional issues. The guide also supports readers coping with illness or injury, experiencing loss and grief, and those searching for meaning as they grow older.

Written in a conversational style, *An Essential Guide to Aging Well* motivates its readers to be curious about this time of life, and to design the best possible version of it for themselves.

**Katharine Bethell, MSW,** was a Board Certified Diplomate in Clinical Social Work. She has 25 years of experience as a psychotherapist treating adults and couples in an outpatient private practice.

"As someone who has the pleasure and privilege of working with older adults, I am grateful that I now have a go-to resource to share with my patients and friends. Katharine Bethell writes with clarity and empathy about the changes we are all likely to encounter as we age, and the practical exercises she offers will gently guide her readers toward a deeper understanding of their individual experiences. *An Essential Guide to Aging Well* provides a refreshing and authentic perspective on aging that I have not found elsewhere, and that I will be encouraging others to read and re-read."

—Jennifer Crumlish, Ph.D., *Washington Psychological Center*

"This book is a capital 'G' Guide to retirement, explaining how retirement can be a valued beginning, not just an ending. By designing the book to mobilize the reader's strengths in facing retirement, Katharine Bethell demonstrates the wisdom and sensitivity that characterized her success as a therapist. This informative, sensible, very readable book is must reading for anyone contemplating retirement—and life after retirement."

—*Allan M. Leventhal, Ph.D.*

"Katharine Bethell, an accomplished psychotherapist, has written a book that is equal parts wisdom, wit, and gentle counsel. Wherever you are on the aging trajectory, this book belongs on your bedside table."

— *Gretchen McKnew, MSW,*
*licensed independent clinical social worker*

# AN ESSENTIAL GUIDE TO AGING WELL

## Older, Wiser

*Katharine Bethell*

NEW YORK AND LONDON

First published 2021
by Routledge
52 Vanderbilt Avenue, New York, NY 10017

and by Routledge
2 Park Square, Milton Park, Abingdon, Oxon, OX14 4RN

*Routledge is an imprint of the Taylor & Francis Group, an informa business*

© 2021 Katharine Bethell

The right of Katharine Bethell to be identified as author of this work
has been asserted by her in accordance with sections 77 and 78 of the
Copyright, Designs and Patents Act 1988.

All rights reserved. No part of this book may be reprinted or reproduced or
utilised in any form or by any electronic, mechanical, or other means, now
known or hereafter invented, including photocopying and recording, or in
any information storage or retrieval system, without permission in writing
from the publishers.

*Trademark notice*: Product or corporate names may be trademarks or
registered trademarks, and are used only for identification and explanation
without intent to infringe.

*Library of Congress Cataloging-in-Publication Data*
A catalog record for this title has been requested

ISBN: 978-0-367-22385-4 (hbk)
ISBN: 978-0-367-22386-1 (pbk)
ISBN: 978-0-429-27461-9 (ebk)

Typeset in Joanna
by Deanta Global Publishing Services, Chennai, India

# CONTENTS

| | | |
|---|---|---|
| | Preface | vii |
| | Acknowledgments | ix |
| | About the Author | x |
| 1 | The Republic of Let's Not Go There | 1 |
| 2 | What Does It Mean? | 5 |
| 3 | How Did This Happen? | 15 |
| 4 | The Rear View Mirror | 23 |
| 5 | The Selfie | 31 |
| 6 | You and Your Role Models | 39 |
| 7 | Decisions: Taking Control, and Letting Go | 49 |

vi    CONTENTS

8   Working. Or Not.                                      57

9   Your Practice, Your Projects                          69

10  Moving. Or Not.                                       81

11  Lighten Up                                            91

12  Do Less. Be More.                                     99

13  Warranty Expiring                                     107

14  Stormy Weather                                        117

15  You and Your Constant Companion                       125

16  The Significance of Others                            131

17  Loves Lost                                            143

18  When It All Falls Apart                               151

19  The View From Here                                    159


Appendix I: Creating A Personal Timeline                 169
Appendix II: Retirement: Making It Happen                171
Appendix III: Talking With Each Other                    173
Bibliography                                             175

# PREFACE

*Katharine Bethell*

If you're like many people, you may not have given a lot of thought to your old age—beyond, perhaps, an occasional fantasy of lying in a hammock in a tropical paradise. This phase of the life cycle may not have seemed very interesting, let alone appealing. But if you're intelligent and curious and you've gone through the years meeting all kinds of challenges, you can do this aging thing well.

Still, it's unfamiliar territory. You deserve a proper introduction to its mysteries. Think of this guide as a conversation with a trusted traveling companion. Advice is offered gently, not prescriptively. The prevailing attitude is positive, but not naïve. Like all good counseling or therapy, the goal is to help you help yourself. To get real about what's happening. To make choices in your own best interest.

I'll begin by asking you to look back and revisit different chapters of your story thus far. Your informal autobiography will reveal a sense of who you are—and what matters most—at this point in your life. You'll find that preparation useful going forward. Then we'll explore a range of topics relevant to aging wisely. Approaching the decision to retire or modify a career and successfully navigating that transition. Making other game-changing choices in the later years. Designing daily routines and engaging in purposeful activities. Connecting with others as relationships shift and evolve over time. Managing moods—the interface of aging with emotional issues. Coping with illness. Sustaining loss and experiencing grief. Searching for meaning.

Real people appear throughout this book; I've changed their names. What do I leave out? I won't mention foods that are alleged to boost your brain power, herbal supplements promising longevity, or the latest cosmetic procedures to minimize wrinkles. I won't offer advice on a more serious concern—financial security in the later years, a subject that deserves its own essential guide.

Most of all, I hope my book will help you overcome your dread or denial of aging. And I hope you will discover that even as your control over various aspects of life is apt to diminish with age, there's much satisfaction—even pleasure—still ahead.

# ACKNOWLEDGMENTS

My deep appreciation to:

Tom Bethell, editor *extraordinaire*. It seems we've stood and talked like this before.

Susan Elliott and Cassie Furgurson, muses and guides.

Lydia Joyner McAvity, trusted advisor.

With thanks for their insights and contributions:

Linda Bennett, Joan Berman, Lanny Berman, Richard D'Amico, Jennifer Elliott, Gary Facente, Pat Furgurson, Vicki Ferenbach, Audrey Francis, Tish Gardner, Greg Lebel, Kevin LeGrand, Sonja Kubota Johansson, Cecile Joyner, Phyllis Kramer, Allan Leventhal, Carol Leventhal, Louise Lusignan, Nikki Gersten McAvity, Barry McCarthy, Gretchen McKnew, Gerry Otremba, Lee Petty, Philip Silverman, Marcus Skeel, Randi Rubovits-Seitz, M.D., Tory Ruttenberg, Susan Vincent, and Mark Willcher.

And thanks to the women of my book club, all ages, all wise:

Brigid, Christina, Claudia, Elizabeth, Gretchen, Jessica, Jo-Ann, Karlyn, Louisa, Mary Ann, Mary Pat, Phyllis and Stephanie.

# ABOUT THE AUTHOR

## *Katharine Bethell*

As a practicing psychotherapist in Washington, DC, for 25 years, Katharine Bethell listened as hundreds of men and women told her their life stories. They shared their secrets, hopes, fears, and dreams; she gave them support and guidance. As she grew older along with her patients, she gained insights into the many issues of aging and an appreciation for the distinctive character of old age, both its perils and its potential pleasures.

Her talent in psychotherapy was the ability to work gently around psychological resistance and defenses, and she brings that quality to her writing. In a conversational style, and often with humor, she addresses topics of aging that typically elicit groans from the over-60 population. Without minimizing the obvious challenges associated with growing old, she opens her readers' minds and hearts to the possibilities that lie ahead. She joins them—as she joined her patients—in a collaboration that honors their best instincts and helps them make intelligent choices about living well in their later years.

ABOUT THE AUTHOR     XI

Katharine Bethell received her M.S.W. degree from Catholic University of America in 1983. At the time of her retirement from clinical practice, she was a Board Certified Diplomate in Clinical Social Work and a Licensed Independent Clinical Social Worker in the District of Columbia.

Over the years she has written countless clinical reports. This is her first book.

# 1

## THE REPUBLIC OF LET'S NOT GO THERE

It's an interesting phenomenon. Most of us, when we were children, couldn't wait to grow up. Think of your four-year-old self, proudly displaying all five fingers on one hand when someone asked how old you were, only to have a parent remind you that your birthday was still a few weeks away. Now that we are full-grown adults, it's the other way around. There are too many candles on that cake. We wish we were young—or at least younger.

Old age as a state of being is a bit like an unappealing foreign territory, a place you wouldn't want to visit—the Republic of Let's Not Go There. It's true that somewhere along the way, usually in middle age, we have a glimpse of what it might be like to grow old, but it's a partial glimpse shrouded in euphemism. There's even a vocabulary designed to take the edge off what is happening. Senior citizens, golden agers, perennials, members of the elderhood—perhaps they are young-at-heart—are said to be living joyfully in their sunset years.

Some of us go to great lengths to avoid the fact of our mortality. Even if we're fortunate and have good models for growing old—relatives, friends, mentors—we still persist, consciously or otherwise, in the belief that old age is something that happens to someone else. Developmentally, we are shielded from this reality for a lovely, long stretch from birth through the young adult years. But somewhere in the middle years, we begin to encounter the disconcerting possibility that we will not live forever.

Rather than experiencing an epiphany of consciousness, we tend to buffer ourselves against the truth of growing old with a variety of strategies. Simple avoidance and outright denial are favorites. Dubious humor—take a look at the birthday cards for folks over 50!—plays its part. Some of the markers along the way are physical, some are cognitive, and some are emotional. They are all signposts on a road that we would prefer not to travel, so we make fun of them or try to ignore them. Old age has been described as a slow, reluctant march into enemy territory. The image makes us nervous.

Still, I refer to "old age" deliberately. The phrase may prompt you to stop reading, but wait a moment. To name something is to make it real. To name something that is personal is to own it. When you make something explicit, you take it out of the realm of the repressed, the ambiguous, and the amorphous, and create a foundation on which to build something of value. So here's the challenge: to overcome your denial, abandon the quest for the fountain of youth and accept the reality that you are growing old. Why? Because that's the first step—claiming your oldness—to living well in your advancing years.

THE REPUBLIC OF LET'S NOT GO THERE

It's curious how seniority in most situations or settings means the recognition of some sort of achievement worthy of respect, if not downright admiration. We honor our veterans. We designate our professors and pastors "emeritus." But when it comes to claiming our advanced position in the life cycle, we're ambivalent. Maybe we're just reluctant, maybe downright resistant. The fact is, we're becoming eligible for membership in a club we never wanted to join.

Many factors influence our ability to accept this new status. Some are personality traits such as our capacity for change, our flexibility or adaptability. As you would guess, health conditions are somewhat predictive, and personal finances play a major part. There's also a family dimension that makes a difference in our openness or willingness to accept our advancing age with a little grace. The memories you hold of older relatives—the hardy grandfather who played catch with you into his 80s or the great-aunt who mailed you postcards from her travels to exotic places—are positive. Less so is the remembrance of an aging parent who struggled with a debilitating illness or a favorite uncle who became withdrawn and irritable. And it's not only our experience with the older generation, but also the attitudes that were passed down. Any indication of respect for old age, tempered with tolerance for its accompanying quirks, counts for a lot in shaping our own attitudes.

It's hard to quantify old age, although social scientists and others try to put brackets around it, even labeling a subset the "oldest old." You've heard the joke that old age is ten years older than you are now. Or that 60 is the new 50, and so on. I was amused to hear someone describe today's "new old age" as the years between feeling fine and being dead. Whether academic or entertaining, these efforts to define old age miss the point. What matters more is your self-awareness, grounded in your experience and enhanced by your insights.

4    THE REPUBLIC OF LET'S NOT GO THERE

Before you bravely lay claim to the title of old person, let's explore what that means. Then we'll take a look at the clues that you may be eligible. And if you're motivated—you've accepted your status and begun to adapt—we'll consider various ways to make the best of it. I'm not saying it's always fun. But you can prevail. You can be older and wiser.

# 2

## WHAT DOES IT MEAN?

Mortality. That dreary word itself is enough to dampen our spirits. Yet a failure to claim—let alone embrace—our mortality has the obvious consequence that we are unprepared for the inevitable. No chance to express what we meant to communicate to people we love, no wrapping up of affairs, no final visits to scenes of our youth or even our middle age. Ironically, to acknowledge that this life has an ending is to open up opportunities—beginnings, in a sense—to live as fully as possible in the time available.

If we're immortal, time is eternal. What's the hurry? Why take risks, try something new, reach out to another person, when there is all the time in the world? Why focus on the quality of life in your last decades, when the decades roll on forever?

But when you think about it, how can you take something seriously if you pretend it's not happening? That's the problem with denial.

If we accept that our stay on the planet is finite, that the supply of time allotted to us is not endlessly renewable, we become motivated to use that time differently. We're already familiar with this phenomenon of deadlines. When our mother said she was going to count to three before losing it, we put our Legos away—fast. When the term paper was due in 24 hours, we wrote furiously. When the boss issued a new drop-dead date for our project, we hustled and delivered. We know how to focus, when it matters.

If we can't be sure how many years we have left, we can choose to use that time wisely. Selectively. No point squandering it on things or people or activities that don't really matter to us. We may also come to appreciate the mere existence of time, knowing that it's not forever. Something to ponder the next time you're stuck in traffic. Can you breathe deeply and be grateful that you are still here on this earth? Even in a backup lasting three lights? No? Give it a try.

You will also discover that time passes more quickly as you grow older. Time acceleration ramps up slowly across the life cycle but really picks up momentum in old age. Do you remember how it once seemed forever to wait for holidays to come around? Now, like birthdays, they reappear with startling frequency. As children, we knew very well the feeling of longing for something to happen, whether it was merely recess or—better yet—the end of the school year. Now that sense of anticipation is abbreviated. On the one hand, we feel the loss of possibility as the clock ticks faster. It's an unwelcome development. On the other hand, what a curious effect this speeding-up can have when the days and weeks no longer stretch before us in such a seemingly endless progression. Life is on fast forward. That's not all bad, if you find that it motivates you to use time wisely.

There's a corollary to this time warp. A much older friend once remarked to my younger self, "You know, aging is a time of rapid change." At the time, I was mystified. In my view, there was nothing amped up about getting older. It looked like reaching a plateau of some sort, flat and rather dull. But she was mostly right about the change part. Better to think of it as strong currents in a river, with occasional rapids to navigate.

## What's Ahead

Much of the change that accompanies aging is physical—outright aches and pains, mysterious twinges, morning stiffness that lasts all day. Much is related to mind and memory—elusive words, forgotten names, misplaced reading glasses. At the very least, we find ourselves disconcerted by these alterations and disruptions to our previously taken-for-granted level of functioning in the world. At our best, we find ways to compensate for diminished stamina or the arrival of the hated, feared senior moment. Some of the adaptation is behavioral—learning to operate within certain physical limitations. Some of the adaptation is cognitive: writing things down instead of committing them to your increasingly faulty memory, coming up with some kind of gimmick to remember the name of the person you met five minutes ago.

The challenge in either category is to revise our long-standing and trusted organizing principles for getting through life, in order to keep on keeping on. I refer to principles as though they were well-defined and explicit, a nice orderly set of guidelines. Actually, during your younger years they were such semi-automatic and habitual patterns of acting and thinking that they required little or no effort on your part. But as you grow older, you'll probably want to make your organizing principles more conscious and deliberate. You may need to gauge the distance from parking place to store entrance before you shop. You may need to design a new ritual to ensure that all the burners on the stove are turned to OFF before you leave home. You may need to ask your new acquaintance to repeat her name and then pair it with some obvious or fanciful image in your mind. That's helpful—some of the time.

If you take a good look at those long-standing principles that have brought you this far, they were probably, to some degree, performance-oriented. Now the determination to do well at whatever you did through much of life is loosening its hold. Of course, people vary, with some hell-bent on excelling and beating out the competition from the fourth grade forward, scoring the most runs on the tee-ball team, winning the essay contest, or landing a seat on the City Council. Others made their peace with this pressure somewhere along the way. But the prevailing emphasis in the younger years is apt to be on comparing yourself to others, and wanting to come out on top. In contrast, one definition of the meaning of old age is this: you get to be yourself. You're less concerned with how others perceive you, more intent on living your own life. It's a departure from youthful insecurities and middle-age uncertainties. Older people can't necessarily tell you when or how they arrived at this point—but it's a good place to be.

In addition to the freedom associated with caring less about others' opinions, old age can mean more free time and fewer obligations. Even with commitments, you may not have to go all in, as you did when you were younger. You can take a break from that volunteer job, or switch one for another. There are trade-offs, to be sure, as your significant others, family members, and dear friends grow older right along with you. They come equipped with their own age-related issues and the need for your support and assistance. It's a balancing act, caring for others and caring for yourself.

## A Touch of Technophobia

The world isn't standing still while you slowly come to terms with your aging process. If you were an early adopter of technological advances, you can relax. You are completely at home on the internet. You understand the cloud, you have more than a dozen apps on your smartphone, and maybe you text with two thumbs. But if you came of age before the revolution, it's not necessarily easy to adapt. As you grow older, the gulf between your analog self and the digital world grows ever wider.

Some claim their oldness as a matter of pride, insisting on books that have hard covers and resisting all invitations to join social media. Their resistance to technology is their way of honoring the way the life used to be, the one they know so well. Just as often, it's driven by a fear of the unfamiliar, the kind of anticipatory anxiety that goes with learning something new. The trade-off, of course, is the opportunity to upgrade your personal operating style and increase your pleasure in life. We'll look into making this a project in Chapter 9.

## Some Gender Differences

In previous generations, the fact of being male or female may have made a more significant difference in the process of adaptation to advancing age. The old stereotype was of a man suddenly faced with the need to pursue new activities—and find a new identity— after he retired from many years absorbed in his work. As women edge toward greater equality in the workplace—and greater job satisfaction—they may face a similar quandary of how to channel their energy post-retirement. But an older woman is apt to have years of experience with multi-tasking and juggling various roles. However committed she may have been to the work she did, her identification with it may have been somewhat less singular than that of her male counterpart. She may have already developed a menu of interests to pursue as she grows older.

Women may have an advantage over men in their ability to anticipate alterations in their bodies as they age. Men and women share in the surprises of puberty, but the female life cycle involves monthly reminders of this maturation until a woman reaches menopause, which offers more evidence that aging is underway. If she chooses to reproduce, she experiences even more physical transitions. For some women, these years of conscious awareness and attention to the body—how it works—helps to ease the adaptation to aging and make it more tolerable, less shocking. The inevitable alterations in appearance are more difficult for many women to accept, as they fear their perceived loss of attractiveness and change of status in the biological mating dance.

As our society places more emphasis on the fluidity of gender roles—and even accepts the possibility of gender transformation—the once-traditional images and expectations of men and women in old age will continue to evolve.

## Similar Experiences

Male or female, what else is likely to occur? The meaning that you assign to all manner of things is up for review. As noted, advancing age can influence your perception of other people's behavior and your reaction to it. Life's slings and arrows may still be aimed in your direction, but you can choose to take them less personally or just dodge out of the way. Once upon a time, a rude remark by a neighbor might have had you brooding for days. Now you may be able to chalk it up to bad manners and shrug it off. Your attitude may become more benevolent; you may forgive more easily.

You may also become more sentimental, more easily touched emotionally. Memories of the past or kindnesses in the present bring tears to your eyes more readily than ever. The same holds true for the utterly predictable ending of a movie, the wedding of people you don't even know very well, the first few bars of the national anthem. Call it sensitivity and take pleasure in your ability to be touched. Your heart softens; you can afford to let your guard down.

WHAT DOES IT MEAN? 11

If you're not so lucky, old habits—resentments, grudges—are reinforced. You become less flexible in your reactions, more rigid in your opinions. But consider that your behavior or your attitude is not so much a matter of being right as it is self-protective. Feeling bad or staying mad is familiar territory. Who knows what will happen if you take a different path? You might feel vulnerable, which can be a scary prospect in old age.

You may also surprise yourself by becoming less acquisitive as your years advance. Some once-passionate pursuits—enhancing your wardrobe, adding to your collection of regional cookbooks or baseballs signed by Major Leaguers—lose their intensity. Sometimes they fade entirely, and you deaccession some of the stuff that surrounds you as you attempt to live more simply. In any case, the trend is in the direction of less rather than more, breaking free from the urge to possess things. The timing is fortuitous. As you grow older, your need for various kinds of practical help is apt to increase. It's going to make sense to budget more for services than for worldly goods. Not as much fun, but realistic.

Old age also means that activities that once seemed trivial are up for reconsideration. You probably never thought that organizing a kitchen shelf or returning a library book was much of an achievement. But as energy declines or vision diminishes or mobility is compromised, you gain a different understanding of what matters and what deserves your respect as an accomplishment. No prize will be awarded for spotting the first crocus or paying your credit card bill on time—but old age means congratulating yourself on noticing your surroundings and on taking care of ordinary tasks. Small pleasures.

Small is the operative word here. When you think about it, you're really coming full circle in old age as your universe grows smaller. Once your environment was the size of a crib. You grew and went out into the world; you explored and expanded your territory. Now the momentum shifts the other way. Maybe you have downsized and moved to smaller quarters. Maybe travel is more daunting, especially if it involves a walker. Maybe your social life is restricted by the passing of old friends. In a variety of ways, your horizons have been narrowing.

## Experiencing Loss

Another transformation in old age is painful, and profound. Grief accumulates. Do you remember when you were young and lost a friend in a terrible accident or a grandparent died? Chances are that the blow occurred in isolation—one trauma to endure—and then life returned to some semblance of normality. There was opportunity for healing. If you were fortunate, considerable time might pass before you would experience another significant loss.

Old age, on the other hand, means that mourning is ongoing. You no longer have the luxury of restoring yourself to an emotional baseline before the next loss occurs. Not only do you suffer when you lose people you love, but you suffer from realizing—not always consciously—that your turn is coming.

When we're young, most of us are somewhat uncomfortable in the presence of loss and grief. What do we say to the bereaved? And if the loss is personal, how should we act? What is normal? Should we be more upset or less, should we show our feelings or hide them? How long should it take to recover?

In old age, grief becomes more familiar. We become somewhat less fearful of it. When loss occurs, it doesn't always upend the natural order of things in the shocking way it did in our youth or even middle age. Rituals and customs can help to comfort and sustain us. Most significantly, we live into author Thomas Lynch's wisdom that grief is the tax we pay on our attachments. We acknowledge and honor the depth of our relationships and the intimacy of our connections as we face giving them up. The real loss would be if we paid no tax. And so we grieve.

## Obviously Not for Sissies

So, what does old age mean? You know the cliché—it's not for sissies. Old age requires us to face all kinds of problems at the very time that our stockpile of resources may be shrinking. Old age brings physical decline, cognitive deficits, and emotional vulnerability. What's the good news when you are experiencing what one veteran old person calls "the dwindles"?

Despite these disappointments and your possible disaffection, there is still much to learn about life and living well. Some discoveries are about the world—note the crocus—and some are about yourself. Either way, the negativity that surrounds aging can all too easily interfere with our curiosity. Better to assume the attitude of an anthropologist observing another culture. Figure out how you relate to this tribe of Older People, a tribe to which you now belong or into which you may soon be initiated. You may even come to agree with the poet May Sarton when she tells us that old age is not interesting—until we get there.

Theories about growing old are useful, at their best illuminating. But the most important meaning of this time of life could be your own. You may think of an advantage or a benefit that is unique to you, very personal, or even private. Stay with this thought for a few moments. See if you can identify something appealing, something that wasn't available in your youth or middle age. If you come up empty this time, revisit the possibility from time to time. The returns are not all in.

# 3

## HOW DID THIS HAPPEN?

The recognition of advancing age dawns slowly for most people. There are inklings from time to time—a stray gray hair or a momentary difficulty getting up from a chair—but you can choose to ignore them. When these signs and portents start to form a pattern, the meaning is harder to escape.

Think about your own clues.

Forgetting a name you know well. Misplacing your keys. Having some trouble reading the menu. Turning the music down so you can hear the conversation. Looking for a bench in the museum. Opting for the elevator instead of the stairs. Entering a room but having no clue about why you went there. Taking more naps. Feeling the cold. Forgetting where you parked your car. Searching for a name you recognize in the list of Grammy Award winners.

Or the annoying ones—nighttime cramps in your legs, strange sparks of light in your eyes, more frequent trips to the bathroom.

And the unmentionables—thinning of hair, lessening of libido.

Other clues worth noting are changes in your personal play-book, the one based on years of developing your preferences and strongly held opinions. Maybe a few prejudices have made their way into it, in a category we might label "I'll never...". When you revise this unwritten script, consciously or otherwise, you are marking a transition from middle age.

Take travel. It was easy to reject the idea of going on a cruise when you were in great shape and looking for adventure. Now, not so much. Or food. If it tasted good, you ate it; now you check the fiber content on the cereal box. Or shoes. Once you endured the misery of high heels; now you're tempted to wear what you and your friends once called old lady shoes.

When you were young, shortcuts were the quickest way to get to school. The focus was on saving time. As you depart middle age, shortcuts are about saving your energy. Some may even earn your approval. Take cooking. Once you were a true believer in the gospel of made-from-scratch; now you try a dish from the prepared food section of the supermarket and find it quite acceptable. Long ago you were taught that a note of thanks had to be a paper-and-pen production; now you send a prompt and sincere email, even a text. Back in the day, you enjoyed your status as the last to leave a party; now you front-end the fun and head home at a reasonable hour.

If you've always been self-sufficient (and proud of it), there's another kind of clue that you're growing older. Just thinking about help—asking for it, accepting it—may be a new development for you, whether you actually give in to the impulse or not. For now, just take note of this shift in consciousness away from your DIY approach to life. Whether your image is of someone else changing a light bulb you can't reach easily, lending a hand with moving heavy boxes, or giving you a very early morning ride to an airport—don't dismiss these possibilities in your future. Think about the occasions when you've been asked to do a favor of some sort. Were you pleased that there was some assistance you could offer to a friend in need—maybe your time, your upper body strength, or your competent driving? It's a bit gratifying to be asked to help. The request becomes an imposition only if you extend yourself beyond what's right for you at that time. As you advance in age yourself, you'll need more help of various kinds—and you'll develop skills at arranging for it.

## The Same, But More So

Not surprisingly, some of the oldness clues are easier to recognize in others than in yourself. You become aware of the "more so" phenomenon in people close to your age. Personality traits may be magnified and typical behavior patterns may be exacerbated. For example, a friend who was always a bit too talkative crosses over into the garrulous zone. Another known for a cavalier approach to making plans becomes even harder to pin down. A sibling who was picky in your childhood years becomes downright obsessive. As for your partner or spouse, you may find that quirks that were once quite endearing and appealing have become irritants, triggers for your frustration.

In conversation with your peers, you may recognize a gradual shift in subject matter. Those same friends who always provided stimulating commentary on world events now lead off with their latest physical setback, diagnosis, or treatment. You may be tempted to join in the organ recital, too. Or they tell long-winded stories about their adorable toddler grandson or their scholarship-winning teen granddaughter. Whatever the subject, it's bound to be repeated. If you're lucky, your friend will offer a preamble, "Stop me if I've told you this before." Most often, you just listen.

You, too, become whatever you have always been—but more so. For example, you may notice that your emotional temperature rises more readily than in the past. Depending on your personality, you may express your opinions more forcefully than ever—at least initially—or mutter to yourself, "I'm too old for this."

The "more so" phenomenon can also pertain to your interests and activities, to the ways you spend time. If you've occasionally indulged in a little daytime TV, you may find yourself lying on the couch binge-watching through a weekend without apology. If you've always loved to travel, you may find yourself making plans to visit a few of the destinations on your bucket list, sooner than anticipated.

There's a variation of the "more so" we might label the do-over. There's a tendency among many older people to want to reread a book they first discovered years ago. To watch a favorite film again—and maybe again. To listen to music in which every note is familiar, or every lyric memorized. There's a wish to reclaim or repeat an experience that is already known and loved.

Of course there are exceptions to the "more so." These take the form of an about-face, a redirection of some sort. Despite the prevailing wisdom that people become more conservative politically as they grow older, you may know someone who surprises you with a ringing endorsement of liberal causes, post-middle-age. Or a people-pleaser who goes all self-absorbed on you. Maybe you find yourself switching from a lifelong immersion in classic literature to downloading bodice-rippers and crime thrillers on your e-reader. We'll encounter this notion of shifting gears or revising attitudes when we read the description of Monica's aunt, one of the role models for successful aging discussed in Chapter 6.

But the trend among most older people is in the direction of acting and thinking and feeling very much yourself, that person you have always been. Just more so.

HOW DID THIS HAPPEN? 19

Also take note of an interesting variety of the "more so" experience that often occurs in families between the generations. As you age, you discover that the gap between you and your parents is closing and you find it easier to identify with them. This holds true whether they are living or have passed away. Women and men talk—sometimes ruefully, sometimes with pleasure—about their enhanced resemblance to a mother or a father as they grow older themselves, how much more like their parents they have become. Maybe it was somewhat apparent in earlier decades. Now the similarities—in mannerisms, in appearance—can be striking.

## Additional Evidence

People of all ages, including strangers, make another kind of contribution to a growing awareness that you're not as youthful as you think—or want to be. They often perceive your changed status before you get the message, and they behave in ways that reinforce your transition out of middle age. A teenager offers you his seat on a crowded bus. A new acquaintance, presumably much older, suggests that the two of you must have graduated from high school in about the same year. Your primary care doctor asks if there are any scatter rugs in your home—not an inquiry about your interior décor but an effort to assess your fall risk. It's as if these people are holding up a mirror for you and you're not sure you want to take a look.

Young children notice signs of your oldness. Without prejudice or hesitation, they affirm it. Annie was as energetic as ever in taking care of her toddler grandson. She was taken aback, briefly, when he asked why she had lines in her face. Tom stepped aside on a sidewalk to allow room for a single file of preschoolers to make their way to the park. When he said "Good morning" to the group, the chaperone prompted her charges to respond. The little boy at the head of the line looked up at Tom and said cheerfully, "Hello, Mister Old Man."

The wider culture plays a part, too, in promoting old age awareness, by offering the senior fare on the bus or the discounted movie ticket or the 5 percent off on Thursdays at the supermarket. An airline wants to sign you up for its Silver Wings program; your gym hopes you will take advantage of its Prime Time offerings. Good deals, maybe, but you may not be entirely pleased about qualifying for membership in these groups—or AARP.

## Tickets of Admission

Not all clues to what is happening are so subtle, lurking outside your consciousness to a degree and thus allowing for some stubborn denial. Life transitions are more explicit markers of admission into the cohort of elders. Big birthdays are obvious examples, the ones that end with "0" or "5." Retirement in any form—from a career, from raising a family, from all kinds of responsibilities—signifies that the aging process is underway. When grown children launch their own adult lives, moving to new locations, choosing partners, and possibly having children of their own, there is a major change in the structure of the family—and your status in it. Perhaps the most profound shift occurs with the death of members of the older generation. As you grieve these losses, you come to understand that your ranking in the life cycle has been moved up. The earlier signposts of maturity—the driver's license, the first real job, a home of your own—those were inconsequential by comparison. Now you are a grown-up. Irrevocably.

Health concerns, of course, play a vital part in this process of coming to admit that you are not getting any younger. For some, the recognition comes as a sudden shock, such as a diagnosis of a potentially life-threatening illness or a prolonged and difficult recovery from a serious injury. For others, the unwanted surprise is that two or more body parts are demanding attention simultaneously. In the past, if you were lucky, you dealt with one physical glitch at a time, and after it was treated you were back to normal. Not now. Medications may multiply, too. Those plastic pill boxes, the ones with compartments marked with the days of the week, once struck you as silly. Not so much, these days.

## Living into It

How did all this happen? It's a normal phase of human development, old age. Consider, as the joke goes, the alternative. To make it more interesting, the average duration of this phase in most parts of the world—the number of years you get to be old—has been extended over the course of centuries. Whether you find it startling or baffling, depressing, or downright comical to enter this stage of life, you are facing a shift in how you think about yourself. It could be compared to the onset of adolescence as an identity crisis, with some distinctive differences. What you see in the mirror changes gradually. Whether your hair is graying or your skin is wrinkling, old age creeps up slowly, in contrast to what seemed like the overnight appearance of breasts in adolescence. The run-up to it takes longer, with two or three decades spent poised in middle age versus the twelve or thirteen years after your birth before puberty hits. The anticipation of it shades to the negative, lacking the excitement of edging closer to the age when you could drive or drink beer legally.

What's important is to claim this evolving image of yourself and live into it, rather than resisting it. "This isn't how I think about myself" is the starting point for most people. It's hard to let go of comparisons. How your neck used to look. How sharp your recall for names and dates was. How few—if any—pills you took. How many miles you could run or how much weight you could lift.

Comparisons are odious. At the very least they are confusing, often misleading, and generally not helpful. You already know that comparing your aging self to your younger self can make you feel bad, or sad, or angry. But the real problem with comparisons is that they take you far from the present moment, which is where you need to be. For now, your job is to just stay open to the possibility that your very oldness is worthy of some attention—and respect.

Once you claim this aging territory as your own, which is another way of saying you have successfully overcome your denial, you can choose your perspective. You'll have to navigate between two poles. At one extreme is the negative attitude that has historically characterized the aging process as dispiriting and debilitating. At the other is a more recent kind of hyper-positivity about growing older that sidesteps the inevitable losses, promotes a sense of joy, and celebrates the presumed vibrancy of your old age. The good news is that it's all on you to make your own sense of the terrain, make your own wise choices. Some day, your indignation at the offer of that seat on a train will be replaced with acceptance—even gratitude.

# 4

# THE REAR VIEW MIRROR

You want to succeed at this age thing. But you can't be good at being old if you're still trying to be young. Youthful, maybe, if that means taking care of your health, exercising, keeping informed about the world, and staying open to new ideas (while retaining the right to reject them after mature consideration). Youthful, if it means looking at the glass half full, at least part of the time. But you've advanced beyond young. If your energy in recent years has been devoted to various age-defying maneuvers and strategies, let's redirect it. Recalling the words of the late sage Ram Dass (as immortalized on countless T-shirts), be here now.

## THE REAR VIEW MIRROR

In order to move on—becoming older, wiser—an emotional journey through your childhood, adolescence, and middle age is in order. You can become the researcher of your own personal history in a project called life review, which is often considered a normal task of late adulthood. It's not to be confused with the kind of near-death life-review experience that people occasionally claim, declaring that "my life passed before my eyes" in an instant. Instead, it's an intentional process of sifting and sorting through your memories of people and places and events, allowing yourself to feel the feelings that are connected to them. It's motivated by the same instinct that causes people to research their family tree or attend their high school reunion. The experience is similar, leading to some unexpected discoveries and a keen sense of your gains and losses over the years.

Engaging in life review helps to integrate your past with your present. As the writer May Sarton has noted, it's like making a map of your world. The more accurately you can draw it, the more clearly you will know where you are now.

### How To Do It

You can review your life quite systematically, working your way through the years, or try a looser approach, associating to various themes.

Let's start with the most structured, the creation of an actual spreadsheet depicting the timeline of your life. The first step is to consider what categories seem relevant to your own story. Some are fairly standard: geographic location, education, work, family. Others are geared to your particular interests over the years: sports, recreation, pets, politics, cultural activities. Major medical events often earn a place on a timeline, as do traumatic experiences. More intimate topics could allow you to track changes in

THE REAR VIEW MIRROR      25

your emotional health and wellness, the evolution of your sexuality or your spiritual life. Once you have chosen your important categories, enter them on the left side of the computer screen—or on a really big piece of paper—in a vertical column. (See Appendix I for an example.)

Across the bottom of the spreadsheet, horizontally, enter the years from your infancy to the present. Grouping them works best: "Birth—Age 5", "Age 5—Age 10" and so on. If you have a good memory for dates and they have meaning for you, you can fill in those specific years as you proceed.

Now take it one topic at a time to create a graphic version of your autobiography. Start with a straightforward category such as Geographic Location. On that line, above the appropriate age ranges at the bottom of the chart, write in all the localities where you have lived. A fairly place-bound person might have made three or four moves in the course of her life. Someone who served in the military or searched to find work during hard times or climbed up the ladder in an organization with many regional divisions might have moved dozens of times. An adventurer or a seeker or a self-described perpetual malcontent might have made the most moves of all.

Entries on the Education line could start with early schooling and continue through the various levels of formal education that apply to you. Include any lessons or tutorials or other educational experiences that are outside that box. If you are taking advantage of any of the programs designed especially for older students—"adult learners"—be sure to note those at the far right of the timeline.

Everyone has some kind of work history. On the Work line, fill in everything from odd jobs in adolescence to your most crowning achievements in later life. Plus everything that falls in between. In the home and out in the world. Paid and voluntary. Memorable and not so much.

26    THE REAR VIEW MIRROR

In the Family category, your entries will reflect changes in the membership of the family you grew up in as well as transitions in your adult life. Chronologically, you might start with the birth of siblings, and proceed through any changes in your parents' marital status and the possible addition of step-relatives. As you grow older on your timeline, note your own status in respect to serious relationships, formalized or not. The same applies to parenting, which encompasses the arrival of children born to you, adopted, or fostered.

All across the Family line, enter the deaths of family members and those important others whom you claim as family.

Follow the same procedure with the more meaningful-to-you categories, the ones you identified that represent your particular interests or concerns.

If you chose Politics, enter the campaign you organized for your friend's election as treasurer of your eighth-grade class. The first time you cast votes in a national election. The age when you began to take issue with your parents' political opinions. The launch of your involvement in local politics, with subsequent wins and losses.

A Recreation timeline is broad in scope, covering pleasurable activities of all sorts. Start with what you loved most as a young child, be it swinging on the playground, playing Clue, or dressing up your stuffed animals in funny costumes. Note what you enjoyed as a teenager, legally or otherwise. Move on to the hobby that you first discovered in your early 30s and still pursue, selecting a few milestones: the pottery mug that wasn't lopsided, the apple pie that won a prize.

It's another kind of venture to track your Emotional Health over the years. For some people, it's mostly a steady state with occasional ups and downs that are hard to capture on a time line. But for others, there are significant events that reflect changes in your mood

THE REAR VIEW MIRROR     27

and behavior at different ages. Diagnosis of a mental health condition, treatment of any kind, self-help efforts—all deserve to be represented here.

When the timeline project is complete, take time to ponder it.

At the very least, this act of remembering is a way to claim what has taken place in your life thus far: the satisfactions, the disappointments, and much in between. See if creating it gives you some sense of coherence, by assembling all the parts in one place.

Perhaps you will find some patterns—such as a series of relationships lasting about two years or a sequence of jobs with bad bosses. Then pay attention to the gaps or missing pieces, and contemplate whether these are lapses in memory or times you would prefer to forget. Be sure to take a close look at how entries in the different categories may be related or have some kind of connection. For example, you may come to find that the summer you were eight years old and were sent to visit your favorite grandmother for a month was the summer your parents separated. Maybe coincidental, maybe not. You could be surprised to find that the year you became more involved in a faith community was about the same time you were coping with a scary medical diagnosis. Perhaps your age when you quit a demoralizing job matches up with the mood improvement you noted on the line that tracks your emotional well-being.

The timeline offers a deliberate and systematic way to take an inventory of your life thus far. You know your style. If you're reasonably organized and somewhat detail-oriented—give it a try.

## A Different Approach

There's another way to take a good look in the rearview mirror. Free association means that you focus on a particular person or place, a specific event or experience—and let your mind roam. Imagine your brain as a computer screen. You've typed in "my uncle," "soccer," "boyfriends who broke up with me," or "employee of the month award." You could have chosen "places I have lived," "embarrassing situations," or "favorite clothes." Or even the big surprises in your life, "unexpected developments."

Get comfortable in a chair and close your eyes. Or, eyes wide open, go for a walk. Sitting or moving, see what comes to mind, without judging or criticizing as you reflect on various parts and pieces of your life story. Try to call up the earliest image or feeling associated with the topic, and then the most recent. Contemplate your most joyful memory and the most humiliating, the funniest, or the saddest, whether you are free-associating to "my birthdays" or "Mom." When you lose focus and your mind wanders to your to-do list or breaking news, explore another chapter heading in your virtual autobiography.

It can be daunting to summon up this personal data that spans decades. All sorts of possessions, your worldly goods, can serve as aids to stimulate your thoughts and feelings. Your memorabilia may be neatly organized into a scrapbook or photo album, or represented by a file of letters you received and saved in those years before email. It could be hanging on your wall, a tidy row of certificates from different phases of your career. Somewhat more random is that bunch of tokens or keepsakes you have collected and housed over the years, each connected to some event or experience in the past. Sometimes the association is obvious, such as the ballpoint pen from the dealership where you bought that beloved car 20 years ago. Others require a bit more effort to track down. At least one object will defy your detective work, like the ashtray with the logo you don't recognize—just an artifact of the long-ago days when you smoked.

You can also consult with family members or significant friends from various eras, when you can't recall something that seems to matter. And internet search engines are always ready to assist you.

## Why It Matters

Much of life review is factual, albeit subjective since you are exploring your own history. But it's also an opportunity to acknowledge and grieve over what hasn't happened in our lives. That our parents never understood who we really were. That we didn't pursue the career we had hoped for. That we didn't get the promotion. That the fantasy of life after our divorce was just a fantasy.

Unmet dreams of every kind. These deserve attention, too, in the form of acknowledging our sadness and disappointment, our frustration and anger.

When your darkest memories include acts of self-destruction, mistreatment or neglect by others, or hurtful circumstances over which you had little control, allow yourself some emotional release. For some people that means writing down their thoughts. For others, a brisk walk or a warm bath. Tears may help. Be kind to yourself.

I'm describing a process that's very internal, but you may involve other people if your recollections are loaded with old regrets and resentments. Even at this late date, you can still tell someone you're sorry or you're angry. If that's not possible, you can write a letter to whomever you offended—or whoever hurt you. Then burn it or bury it or put it through the shredder.

Your life review may also stimulate thoughts of people for whom you feel great affection. Whether these are old friends you haven't seen for years or pals you see every Friday evening, let them know their importance to you. You may live for many years and they may, too—but why not communicate your fondness, your gratitude, right now? One day it will be too late.

Along the way, be sure to remember and celebrate the good times. Smile at some memories; laugh out loud at others. Play the music you love, watch old movies, reread the book that meant so much when you were a senior in high school.

There's no score, no pass-fail. You've created a thoughtful consideration of your life thus far, and a preparation for the discoveries—welcome and not—of old age. I've described it as though it unfolds all of a piece, like a spreadsheet, but that's not really true. Some of life review is spontaneous; some is intentional. Whatever form it takes, however extended or intermittent the process, make it matter. Spend time with it.

This looking back through the rearview mirror has its detractors, those who disdain "living in the past." But the point is to visit the past, not to get stuck there. The point is to recognize and honor the paths you have trod, the places you have been, and the people who have traveled with you on the journey. The point is to understand where you are now.

# 5

# THE SELFIE

At this point in life, how well do you know that woman or man whose reflection you see every time you look in the mirror? Could there be any good reason to spend valuable time and emotional energy getting to know that person even better?

You may not think so. For starters, you may well associate self-absorption with adolescence, a developmental phase from which you graduated long ago. Or you may simply frown on such preoccupation with yourself as indulgent. Egocentric. Even narcissistic. It's entirely possible that when you were growing up, terms like "self-actualization" or "self-empowerment" had yet to enter the conversation, for better or worse. Social media as a means to promote your personal opinions didn't exist. The selfie had yet to be invented, let alone perfected—if that's the word—with the addition of the selfie stick.

32 THE SELFIE

Set aside your skepticism for a moment. A healthy degree of self-awareness is a valuable resource as you go forward in life. If you have embarked upon some form of life review as suggested in the previous chapter, you've made a head start. You've already constructed a map of your world, surveying the terrain and noting your life's significant events. Now let's place you on that map and think about who you are in the here-and-now. Even if you've never been inclined to introspection, let's take a psychological selfie.

The older you are, the greater the wealth of material about yourself. You have many years of life experience that inform your personality. You have suffered and succeeded, lost and gained. As a child, your identity was shaped to a considerable extent by the needs and perceptions of others. Parents were primary, of course, but other authority figures and peers made contributions, too. Over the years, some adults achieve a degree of detachment from those influences and grow into a personal identity that is more distinctively and authentically their own. Others feel that their subjective sense of themselves has remained constant throughout life, with no significant revision over time.

Let's say the description of who-you-are has remained pretty consistent. When you were growing up, your siblings complained that you were stubborn, and it's true, even now. When you were 11, you donated your birthday money from your grandmother to a homeless shelter; friends today say you are the most generous person they know. As a child, you were always anxious meeting someone new; in later life, it takes you ample time with drink in hand before you can relax and enjoy the encounter.

By contrast, you may be someone whose self-image has been altered—even transformed—for reasons known or unknown, the convergence of many circumstances and life experiences. Once gregarious, now you've become reticent in social situations. Once a committed liberal, now you're more conservative—or the other way around. Once rather culturally refined, now you read celebrity mags without shame.

Whether you find that your sense of a personal identity has remained constant as you have aged or has evolved—gradually or even suddenly—you can draw on this information about yourself to help you live well in your later years. Keep in mind that many of the demands and constraints of young adulthood and middle age are being lightened or lifted as you grow older. This works both ways—fewer responsibilities can leave some people feeling emotionally adrift—but in a general sense, aging means increasing freedom to set your own course, to take less responsibility for others and more for your own self. You can make choices, determine your own priorities, and shape your connections to other people in some liberating and possibly satisfying ways.

Whatever your characteristics or personality traits—from iconoclast to solid citizen, from predictable to flighty, from laugh-out-loud funny to solemnly serious—this knowledge of yourself in the present moment forms the basis for making intelligent decisions going forward. By intelligent I mean life-enhancing. Older, wiser.

Some would question such an upbeat scenario. How can you maintain any sense of optimism when the aging process involves some physical and cognitive decline, if not downright impairment? True enough. But consider that a loss of energy or mobility or memory makes it even more essential to create a life that is as consistent as possible with your values, your tastes, your preferences of all kinds. You want the time that is still ahead to be rewarding. And by being selective, you maintain a sense of control over what can be controlled, even as advancing age inevitably alters the equation.

## Getting To Know You

So let's indulge in some introspection, to bring a little clarity to your self-analysis. It's a fairly simple matter—really, you interviewing you. There's no particular format for this inquiry beyond raising questions that cover a variety of topics and giving honest answers.

It's best to start with some issues related to your personal preferences and interests. For example, how do you really feel about a particular individual, that cousin you have known forever? Where would you love to live, if cost were no object—or can you imagine moving elsewhere? What is your favorite way to spend time? Your least favorite? Do you prefer to be alone or part of a group? What do you prize most about your family and what do you resent? Do you like dogs or cats or tropical fish? What do you really enjoy in art or music and what do you ignore? What do you like to read—or, honestly, do you like to read? What foods do you love and which do you spurn? Do you care about fashion? What about TV sports? You get the idea.

Just see what comes to mind. Don't look back in time at how you once felt about these subjects; don't project into the future what you think you *should* feel. Let your imagination roam, fine-tuning your awareness of your likes and dislikes.

Then turn even more introverted with your questions. What do you like best about yourself? And second best? What's a bit embarrassing or hard to handle about your personality? How much do you care about your physical appearance? What are some of your beliefs, be they philosophical or political, arcane or commonplace? Do you tend to act deliberately or spontaneously? Are you trusting or skeptical by nature? Do you have a sense of humor or do you depend on others to make you laugh? Do you consider yourself a genius, just average, or not very brainy? Are you a dreamer, a realist, or somewhere in between? Are you inclined to be a saver or a spender? Would you rather be a host or a guest? Are you mostly confident or do you tend to be insecure? How about empathy for others—does it come easily or do you have to make an effort?

Sometimes the clues are in your behavior, if you take a little time to analyze it.

Joe was opinionated. He had no trouble defining what he believed about the state of the world—and promoting those views with anyone who would listen. He was much less familiar with his own psyche, that funny mix of distinctive characteristics that define a personality. His first experience of raising his psychological self-awareness took place at the gym. He kept noticing that the guy on the treadmill next to his was running at a much faster pace than he was. Joe's insight #1: "I guess I have to admit, I'm very competitive." As he was ending his workout, he spotted someone fumbling with the settings on a rowing machine. Since he knew that piece of equipment well, he offered his assistance. He didn't make much of the moment until he was driving home, when it occurred to him: "In some situations, I get a kick out of helping others." Not exactly an epiphany, really, but good information about himself to file away for future use.

But maybe you're quite aware that this sort of open-ended reflection with your inner self as the subject matter has little appeal. It won't work for you. In that case, you might do better using one of the scores of ready-made personality tests on the market, easily available online or included in many books on the self-help shelf. These are systematic efforts to assess your strengths and your talents along with potential areas for personal growth. Most of them are knock-offs of the well-known Myers-Briggs Type Indicator, which is administered in many settings to help distinguish personality types. The MBTI was originally devised as a non-judgmental way to improve interpersonal dynamics in the workplace; over time, the instrument and its offspring have been used by millions of people as tools for self discovery. There's a big market out there. You can find out which of sixteen personalities is yours, you can investigate which Greek goddess or god you most resemble, you can even complete a questionnaire that will determine which animal you most resemble.

A common criticism of these instruments is that they fail to discern nuances of personality traits. For example, on a scale of

36 THE SELFIE

extroversion and introversion, most adults fall somewhere between the poles. Defining yourself as one or the other doesn't capture your unique blend of those sensibilities. If you do play around—and it can be fun—with any of these self-help quizzes, take what you need but ignore the rest. If there is a useful insight, file it away; if the term or label just doesn't fit, forget it.

Sadie was reluctant to take what she viewed as a test, an evaluation of her strengths and—all too likely, in her mind—her weaknesses. A younger friend who worked in her company's human resources department knew all about these inventories, and convinced Sadie to try an online version. Throughout her adult life, Sadie had been intimidated by people who could assemble an arsenal of facts to support their views on just about any subject. The results of her "test" were enlightening. In the decision-making category, those people who were labelled "Thinking" were described as consistent and logical in their approach, driven by objective data. In contrast, the "Feeling" style accurately captured Sadie's instinct to take people and their emotions into consideration. Neither way of making decisions was deemed superior to the other, just different. Sadie was surprised, and pleased at the validation.

## Why It Matters

Whether it takes the form of an extended off-the-cuff interview with yourself or a structured exercise, any attempt to enhance your self-awareness has value. At any age, it has the potential to reinforce your personal status quo, giving more definition or substance to your self-image. But as you grow older, this inquiry can help to effect some actual changes in the way you live life. For example, honest self-analysis can lead to reevaluating relationships—admitting that you like the company of some people and not others, and revising your social life accordingly. It can mean withdrawing your energy from a particular cause or organization and investing it elsewhere. It can mean admitting that you never liked classical music, however hard you tried, freeing you to tune in to the bluegrass channel from this day forward. It can mean taking inventory of your character flaws and deciding that you'll work to improve in some areas but claim the others as yours to keep.

In the later decades of life, this information has the potential to guide some important decision-making. When reminiscing, you realized how eager you were to meet your tentmates at summer camp, and how much you loved living in a college dorm. Further reflection yielded the insight that your personality is more outgoing than reserved. You may be a good prospect for another pass at communal living, some kind of senior living situation where residents share common spaces and socialize freely.

Maybe the psychological selfie helped you become more keenly aware of your relationship with money. You are beyond frugal, maybe a miser. Family members have been urging you to take some of your savings and indulge in a luxury cruise "while there's still time." But that's not who you are. The security of a savings account means more to you than any bucket-list adventure. In fact, you keep no such list.

Or you affirmed your long history with some deeply held political opinions that differ from those of nearly all of your close companions. Sometimes you've argued, sometimes you've kept quiet, but the tension persists and it does no favor to your blood pressure. Perhaps the better part of wisdom at this age is to let go of the effort to persuade people to adopt your views. You can stay true to yourself and focus only on things you have in common.

Perhaps you acknowledged your fondness for painstaking precision in all of your endeavors. So let people call you fussy. You've aged out of worrying about how others perceive you or trying to live up to certain norms. You have life experience. Along the way you have developed a style of living that, for better or worse, is distinctively your own. Honor it.

## THE SELFIE

Can you change who you are, even as you grow older? Yes. It's more challenging than when you were younger, when the brain was more plastic and habits less ingrained. But unless your core self is rigidly antisocial or aggressively hostile, let's pay tribute to who you are in the present moment. You've worked on becoming this person for many years. Maybe you've arrived.

## Looking Ahead

We associate the term "identity crisis" with earlier phases of the life cycle. Adolescents experiment and flounder as they attempt to define who they are on the brink of their adult lives. The midlife crisis has men—and, increasingly, women—attempting to recapture their youth or somehow compensate for what they have missed along the way. By contrast, the quest for identity in old age is charged with neither the vulnerability of the teenage years nor the urgency of the middle years. Now you are seeking consolidation, some clarity in describing who you have become. Make it a mix of personality factors and character traits. Include your virtues, your quirks, your values. Toss in the superficial things that annoy you. Most importantly, declare the things that you love.

You don't have to work all of this self-awareness into a memoir, although there's nothing wrong with that. At the least, you want to create a record of some sort so the details of your autobiographical excursion won't be lost. The written word is fine, whether it's a hard copy or a digital document saved to the cloud. Or make an audio version on your phone's recording app. However cryptic or expansive your observations may be, you'll have them, to review and revise when further insights come to you. Think of your self-awareness as an asset—one of the resources that will help you resolve some of the dilemmas you'll encounter in the territory of aging.

# 6

## YOU AND YOUR ROLE MODELS

You've been looking in the mirror. Now let's widen your perspective.

We all have people we look up to, men and women from whom we learn how to go about this business of living. Sometimes the lessons they provide are focused and specific, such as teaching us a foreign language or showing us how to change a flat tire.

But maybe we simply admire people for their style or skill. Perhaps we envy their competence or respect their accomplishments. These models don't have to be labeled as mentors or teachers. They can be friends or relatives with whom we are acquainted, celebrities we read about or talk-show hosts we watch on television.

What all these people have in common is their ability to impress or inspire us, to make us want to be a little like them.

## 40    YOU AND YOUR ROLE MODELS

To serve as a model for something, you need to have a role. Here's where oldness enters in. There are no awards or trophies given for Outstanding Old Person, but that's the role that has relevance—and deserves your attention—as you advance in age yourself. Naturally there are many negative images of Old Person, and you are right to reject them. But there's a good chance that you can claim at least one positive role model for your old age if you give it some serious thought. The idea is to make whatever resides in your subconscious a little more explicit so you can make good use of it. More than a few women and men are surprised at what they find when they explore their mind's inventory of not-so-young people who have made a significant mark or impression on their lives. If that doesn't work for you, start now. Make it a project to identify at least one older woman or man whose attitude or approach to life you admire. It's also possible to turn a disappointing or depressing example to your advantage, when you vow not to resemble that unhappy person.

Some models are people you have known for a long time, so you've watched their aging process closely. Others are less personal connections, people you've admired from afar. Take former president Jimmy Carter, for instance. It's hard not to be inspired by a video clip of the 95-year-old volunteering with yet another Habitat for Humanity project, wielding a nail gun.

When you think about role models, try not to be distracted by the resources that they may have. Instead, what matters are the personal characteristics that describe or define them. Does she or he bring a positive attitude to growing older, or possess some attribute that contributes to success in old age? Think how a particular approach to life—or aspect of a personality—might influence your own scenario for aging wisely.

Sources of inspiration are likely to vary widely. Let's look at some examples.

Ashley is in her 50s, but as a young girl she became fascinated by Queen Elizabeth. Ever since, she has been a serious fan of the monarch:

*The queen is not afraid to be her age. She seems so resilient, whatever comes her way. There's nothing trendy about her. People say she's outmoded but I love her way of upholding traditions with such dignity. I would like to be a little like her, even though I'll never wear a crown.*

Judy's role model for aging well is someone she knew for 50 years before the friend's death from cancer. Nora was her "go-to" person when she was troubled, the confidante who could be counted upon to provide perspective and bring humor to most situations. Even close to the end:

*I went to visit Nora a few days before she died. But as I was about to enter the house, I met someone leaving whom I didn't recognize. She introduced herself as a minister. I found this quite strange, since Nora was a lifelong atheist. I went on into the house and saw what a terrible condition my friend was in. I could barely contain my emotions, but instead of crying I said, "Now really, Nora, what was a minister doing here? You're an atheist. What in the world could you say to her?" She replied, in her typically droll style, "I didn't have to say anything to her. I just let her do all the talking." I would have been quick to take offense in that situation. Nora's attitude is an inspiration to me.*

Harriet's grandmother Amy was a hard-working farm wife who raised five children. Along with all her other chores over the years, she baked all the bread for the family. No store-bought loaves on their table:

# YOU AND YOUR ROLE MODELS

> *I always went to see her when I came home from college. One time,*
> *I found her in the kitchen. She was excited. "Look," she said, ges-*
> *turing to yeast and water in a mixing bowl, "I've discovered a new*
> *way to make my dough rise!" I've always remembered that scene,*
> *hoping that I could be so willing to try new things when I grow old.*

Timothy is proud to have his grandfather's name, Norman, as his middle name. His grandfather died when Tim was only 15 and he still misses him today, many decades later:

> *He was never in good health. He had helped build the Panama*
> *Canal when he was in the army and contracted yellow fever, result-*
> *ing in respiratory issues throughout his life. But what I remember*
> *most is that, even dealing with the difficulties of his health, he*
> *always had a sense of humor. Always! I loved that about him. Now*
> *I realize what a gift that was, to his grandchildren. I hope I can*
> *emulate that aspect of him as I get older.*

John remembers his father as a kind but imposing figure who had strongly held opinions on, well, just about everything. Despite the family's concern about his safety and that of others, John's father was still driving his car on winding country roads at age 91:

> *One day my father came home from driving somewhere and handed*
> *his car keys to my mother. It turned out that a tricycle had been left*
> *at the edge of the road. He didn't see it, and he sideswiped it. "I am*
> *so relieved," he announced. "There could have been a child on that*
> *tricycle. There wasn't, thank God. But I know it's time for me to stop*
> *driving." I wonder if I'll be so realistic and decisive if I live that long.*
> *I sure hope so.*

Many of the qualities we admire in a role model—and might want to emulate—are consistent with our image of that person. He or

YOU AND YOUR ROLE MODELS 43

she has seemed thoughtful or funny or determined or empathetic as long as we have been acquainted, whether it's someone we actually know or a public figure. But occasionally there's a surprise, and it's the late-in-life behavior that we find admirable. Cynthia described her father's transformation:

> My father spent most of his life as an anxious, rather shy person. Not very generous with his family, he was often irritated with his noisy, obstreperous children. When both my parents were in their 70s, my mother was laid low by Alzheimer's—and my father underwent a shift in his personality. He was not in the least ashamed of his wife's increasingly odd behavior. He took amazingly loving and gentle care of her in their home until she died at 80. During that period he satisfied his boundless interests about the world through reading and public television. He became very outgoing and people loved to be with him.
>
> A few years after my mother died, my father married a woman who loved learning and travel as much as he did. Together they ranged far and wide around the globe. He died at age 92 as they were planning a trip to Antarctica. His curiosity and his remarkable ability to change are what I admire most.

Not all role models for aging have so many stamps in their passports, or enjoy the company of others to such a great extent. As she exits middle age, Barbara is able to reflect, sadly, on her mother's experience of aging—and to chart a very different course for her own life:

> My mother had a long history of isolating herself socially and it didn't get better as she advanced in age. I remember when she married her fourth husband and moved back to the area where she grew up. Her best friend from childhood still lived there, yet Mother never reestablished contact with her. When she was widowed again and moved into a retirement community, she wouldn't leave her

## YOU AND YOUR ROLE MODELS

*room to take her meals with other people, or to participate in group activities. Instead, Mother expected me to come by every day after I left work, to chat and pay attention to her. In her last five years, she was almost completely dependent on me, my sister, and her doctor for social interaction.*

*I am blessed with a wide circle of friends. I value my connections to many members of my family. I have learned so much from my mother's behavior, the example she set. I am determined not to repeat it.*

Liz offers a touching tribute to a positive role model and mentor, a friend who was in her 60s when they first met:

*My husband and I moved from the city to the country when we were in our 40s. With no experience beyond tending a tiny patio with a few geraniums, we suddenly owned a rather large expanse of garden. Then we met Roberta. Her garden was big and unruly, full of exotic—to us—plants and shrubs. She was generous with her knowledge. I became her acolyte as we wandered around and she educated me about the joys of horticulture, the beauty of different flowering wonders.*

*My parents had died young. I had no model of an older friend outside a work setting. As we slowly shared our lives, I learned that Roberta had lost her husband to a terrible car accident and her first-born son to an illness at age 3. These tragedies informed but did not define her life.*

*As Roberta reached her 80s, she developed Parkinson's but refused to become her affliction. She remained the best company, caring friend, keen observer of the lives around her. As I age into my 70s, I think about her constantly and wish that her example of a long life might guide mine.*

In some relationships, the older person's influence takes the form of outright advice. If guidance turns peremptory or patronizing,

YOU AND YOUR ROLE MODELS        45

we're apt to resist. But when advice is offered gently but firmly, with loving intent, we can accept it. Best of all, it's a gift that keeps on giving long after the source has passed away. When Stephen was 25, he went to work at a small non-profit organization. Ben was his boss:

> I only worked for Ben full-time for a few years, but I stayed in close touch until he died 50 years later. I knew everyone in his family, which sort of became mine. He was my true North, representing what I think of as the best values and hopes for the world, and always acting with integrity. Of course he wasn't perfect. He had a temper and you didn't want to get on his wrong side. But his generosity is what I will remember.
>
> Ben always used the same intro when he had some advice for me: "You need to..."
>
> I needed to read a book he recommended, or I needed to reconsider some half-formed political opinion, or I needed to push myself to take on some new challenge. I can still hear Ben's soft southern voice, guiding my decisions and encouraging me to do whatever he thought I needed to do. He's always right.

As a teenager, Alexandra loved to spend time with her best friend's mother, Mrs. Murray. Mrs. Murray was probably not a day over age 45, hardly an old woman, but to Alexandra she was not only advanced in years but also a model of the kind of empathy that was in short supply in her own family. Over time, the older woman invited Alexandra to call her by her first name, but she politely declined. Mrs. Murray would always be Mrs. Murray:

> I grew up in a very conservative religious tradition. I had different phases: trying to comply with all the rules, rebelling against them, trying to sort out what I really believed. One afternoon when I was probably 15 or 16, I confided in Mrs. Murray, admitting to my confusion and disenchantment with my family's insistence that I adhere

to their brand of religion. Coming from the same faith, she could have disapproved. Instead, she said simply, "Well, just stay open to it." Stay open to it. Over the years—now I'm 76—I'm still trying to follow her advice.

Celebrating his 60th birthday, Jerry turned thoughtful about the occasion, seeing it as a turning point from which he could glimpse his old age (which he likes to describe as his dotage). He's happily married, but admits that his worst fear is loneliness, the possibility of facing the later years of life without a partner. Jerry envies and admires a long-time friend who lives a satisfying life as a single man:

Despite being a good decade or more older than I am, Gus keeps his calendar jam-packed with activities and events. I've learned I can't call him at the last minute and expect him to be available. He makes an occasional vague reference to a serious relationship in the distant past, but without the wistfulness you might expect or imagine. Gus often invokes the memory of his great aunts in mid-century Chicago, who were all widows and led full, vibrant lives. I think they're his role models. Gus is mine, if I ever have to live alone.

Jerry describes another important figure in his life, a positive role model at a difficult time:

Professor Hermann—as I always knew him and still think of him— was a senior faculty member whom I met my freshman year in college. He taught mathematics to very smart people but I avoided taking class with him so I wouldn't be a disappointment as a student. I cherished our social connection and was dazzled by his talents as a skilled furniture maker and accomplished musician. He had a 10-foot Steinway grand piano in his living room!

I adopted Professor Hermann as my first gay mentor and role model. I probably took advantage of his friendship with late-night

YOU AND YOUR ROLE MODELS   47

*calls of complaint and despair, but he never turned me away. He was a strong shoulder during my coming out years when my parents were busy being horrified. Now that I'm getting older myself, I can appreciate the example he set for aging well. Along with everything else he gave me.*

Joanne was in her 20s, single, tackling the challenges of her first real job and life in a big city. She became friendly with her much older neighbor, a retired art teacher who lived down the hall:

*At first I thought Edith must be 102, but of course she was only in her late 70s. I was flattered that she took such an interest in me. One day she invited me in for coffee and asked if I would like to see her latest art project. She had it spread out on a big table. On a large sheet of heavy paper she had written—in beautiful script, almost like calligraphy—the important details of her life to that point. She had drawn details of leaves and flowers between the paragraphs, and a beautiful border around the whole thing. I've never forgotten that moment, when I suddenly realized she was sharing her obituary. I was so impressed, that she could face the ending of life with such clarity, such acceptance. I hope I've taken the lesson to heart.*

"Curiosity about the world"—that's the phrase that occurs so often when people reflect on their role models for aging well. Kenneth spoke about his friend Keith, who was well into his 60s when they first met: "Until his death at age 92, he was engaged with life and he was always eager to make a new friend. He remained curious about the world, to the end." Marian shared thoughts about her father-in-law: "I'm too easily frustrated by some of his quirks. But I can't help admiring the way he's grown older. He's so curious about the world, he's even an early adopter of technology I'm just now learning about."

One positive role model qualifies for the title by taking a short walk every day at age 94, whatever the weather. Another copes with his failing health without feeling sorry for himself. Others maintain their sense of humor, sophisticated and witty or making bad puns the way they always have.

The honor also goes to those who adapt to their circumstances and demonstrate a late-in-life capacity for change. These are role models who defy the conventional wisdom of becoming more set in their ways as they age. Monica described the evolution of her aunt's personality: "She was pretty uptight when I was growing up, quite intimidating. As an old lady, she's less formal, more relaxed, more accepting of all kinds of people. I'm not sure she's conscious of that, but it's so nice to watch someone move in that direction."

Many of the qualities we admire in older men and women are grounded in their realistic attitude toward aging. That realism takes many forms. Maybe it's practical: having the ability to plan ahead but being willing to revise the plan as energy dictates, or recognizing that what used to happen in no time at all—like getting dressed—now takes an hour. Maybe it's a kind of acceptance: the woman who colored her hair for years and decides to go gray, the man whose balance was increasingly precarious until he swallows his pride and acquires a cane. Maybe it's about the future, looking ahead and talking openly about the end of life: the parent who makes her wishes clear, the older friend who asks you to speak at his memorial service when that day comes.

There's no one set of instructions for becoming a role model for aging well. But such women and men are out there, and we do well to notice them and let them guide us. You can take what you need for inspiration. Keep your role models in mind as you proceed on your own journey. Eventually, you can create your own version—becoming an Outstanding Old Person yourself.

# 7

# DECISIONS

## TAKING CONTROL, AND LETTING GO

As more candles are added to your birthday cake, some of your scenarios for the future are likely to be up for revision unless you're blessed with a large inheritance and perfect health. The possibilities—how you spend time and with whom, where you live, how you get around—are not quite as open-ended as they once seemed. Because it's a good bet that at least one of your resources is diminishing. It could be emotional energy or physical stamina. It could be time. It could be money. The older you become, the more these limitations affect your ability to choreograph life to your liking.

Naturally, some of the choices you made in the past have a profound influence over the options available as you grow older. As Fred Astaire (among others) is alleged to have said, "Old age is like everything else. To make a success of it, you've got to start young." That seems to have worked out well for Fred, but few among us had any clue, way back then. Now it may be that the best you can do is to make this connection between past experience and present options more explicit.

It's important to accept that certain possibilities were precluded long ago. You got an education or specialized training, or you didn't. You jumped through various career hoops, or you didn't. You became a parent, or you didn't. These decisions are somewhat immutable, past the age of 60. You can audit college courses, you can develop an "encore career," you can volunteer to teach young children how to read. All well and good. But except for some possible detours, most of us are traveling pretty close to the same road we set out upon a long time ago.

Let's give special attention to the choices you made in good faith—or innocence—that haven't held up very well. Perhaps you chose to be coupled but ended up single. Or you moved into your forever home and found you couldn't afford it. Add to this list the choices with repercussions over a lifetime that would have been hard to imagine, back in the day. Marrying a much older spouse. Moving far away from family members. Choosing a career based in a technology that became obsolete before you retired.

Much of your decision-making in youth and middle age was probably guided by an informal consideration of the ratio of costs and benefits. For most of us, not a very deliberate process. If you took risks, you figured that at some level you had the strength of spirit and the resources to revamp and revise as necessary. You could bear the costs.

If you didn't take risks—and with hindsight, wish you had—you need to treat yourself gently. Have you ever realized that you did the best you could at the time, given the synergy of your circumstances and your fears? Give yourself some credit. Besides, you don't really know what the outcome would have been if you had acted more boldly or courageously, if you had been more ambitious or adventurous. In your fantasy, you field reporters' calls after learning you've received a MacArthur genius grant. Could happen, but what are the odds?

If living well in old age means bringing some selectivity to bear on the choices that remain, what then? A first step is sorting through the old ones, to recognize the frustrating or disappointing choices that can't be made over, not at this time in your life.

This is hard work, to be so honest with yourself. If you can find some saving grace, some unexpected satisfaction that emerged from a bad decision, that's fine. It's more likely that you'll end up grieving for the man or woman—you—who made those choices long ago. It's tempting to judge that young and inexperienced person by the standards of your older, wiser self. That's not fair. Instead, summon your empathy and try to forgive yourself.

Not easy. But you deserve some relief if you are weighed down by bags full of regrets when you make excursions into your past. Better to save your emotional energy for what's ahead.

## Taking Control

What are some of the dilemmas typically associated with advancing age? There's your work life: if, when, and how to retire, and what to do thereafter. And your living situation: downsize or not, age in place or move to a retirement community, stay in familiar surroundings or relocate near family members. Health issues: if, when, or how to change doctors, to seek a second opinion, to opt in or out of elective procedures. Financial decision-making: save or spend, shop with coupons or treat the whole family to a luxury vacation, if you can afford it. And all those baffling considerations related to driving your car: daytime only, perhaps, or sticking to familiar routes, or—reluctantly—turning in your keys.

Whatever the problem you are trying to solve, you may be surprised by your sense of caution. A certain degree of risk aversion often goes with the aging process. This trepidation can be trumped, of course, if you're willing to adopt "if not now, when" as your mantra. To do that means accepting the trade-off of downside and upside, gambling that you can tolerate the former in hopes of enjoying the latter. Adoption of this stance is grounded in your understanding that life won't be affording you these options forever.

Whichever group you belong to—a bit fearful or going for broke—you can master the art of dealing with life's possibilities in a way that improves the outcome of your decision-making. To start, put some time and thought into defining the issue you are trying to resolve. You want the fullest possible description of the problem at hand. Consider making a list and writing down all the variables. Explore the quandary, whatever it may be—profound to seemingly trivial—until you've identified as many angles as possible. If you find that you are looking not at one issue to resolve but at several, that's a useful discovery.

When you can't think of another detail to add, focus on the consequences—the benefits and costs—of each potential resolution of the situation you are addressing. Your age works in your favor as you bring an accumulation of self-knowledge to this process, pondering each possibility in regard to its suitability for you. Keep in mind that you are assessing what's appropriate in the here and now. Keep the memories of what was once right for you at bay; keep your fantasies of the future under some control.

Then use your creativity to bring all this analysis to a satisfying conclusion. Of course, some questions can be answered with a simple Yes or No. But consider that your reward may be to find a solution that's outside the original box. Perhaps your decision will involve phases or stages of action rather than a focus on a single point in time. Maybe you'll think of a substitute for some part of the puzzle that seemed unsolvable, at the outset. You may even experience a shift in the importance that you give to the problem under consideration, granting it less significance in the great scheme of things.

Let's look at some real-world examples.

Marie was diagnosed with multiple sclerosis in middle age. She coped well, relying on her resilient spirit. But as she aged, her symptoms were exacerbated. As a meticulous housekeeper, it pained her to let go of her high standards and face the reality that she couldn't live up to them. She found dirty windows especially depressing. One day she took fresh stock of her situation. She reconsidered the problem, thinking about all of her windows, throughout her house; she rethought her options beyond clean or not-clean. She made the choice to clean one particular window until it sparkled, and to especially enjoy looking through that opening to the outside world.

Roy, a successful man in his early 70s, was increasingly troubled as he faced the decision to resign from his accounting firm. He loved the work that had defined and supported him for decades. On the other hand, it was hard to ignore the fact that the firm's junior partners were the same age as his grown children. Long-time colleagues were retiring all around him. To resolve the issue, he adjusted his focus beyond staying versus leaving. He began to wonder if there were alternatives to life at the firm, other ways to maintain his professional identity and share his expertise. He explored various possibilities, from part-time consulting to a volunteer job teaching the fundamentals of accounting at the local community college. He found he could "retire" and add to his résumé at the same time.

Natalie lost her husband after a long illness. She was caught between well-meaning friends who urged her to relocate to a nearby retirement community as soon as possible—for her safety and well-being—and others who insisted that it was folly to make such a big decision in the first year following her spouse's death.

She seesawed between moving and staying in her own home, and her anxiety spiked. When she reworked the definition of her dilemma, she began to find some clarity. She made notes about her hopes and her fears in this life transition. She joined a support group for widows and widowers, seeking guidance from people who didn't know her and didn't have their own strongly held views of what she should do. She researched cooperative living possibilities. Before long, the decision ("What should I do?") gave way to a process that she could pursue ("What matters to me now and what living situation would best support it?"). She made a thoughtful choice, ten months later.

Important celebrations—holidays, birthdays, graduations, vacations, reunions—present all kinds of opportunities to revise your decision-making in an older, wiser mode. Maybe you've upheld traditions of long standing, rituals loaded with meaning to you and significant others. The very thought of making changes is unsettling, at best.

Ruby, a devoted mother and grandmother widowed in her 70s, had a positive outlook on life and was grateful to be in good health. Still, she approached the Christmas season with trepidation. She simply lacked the energy to make the holiday live up to the expectations of the family members who had always counted on her, year after year, to create a festive environment, arrange for entertainment, and feed them all well.

On an occasion fraught with so many memories, she knew that any revision of the family's time-honored routines should start small. She admitted she had no idea how others would react, but she was determined. So she acquired all the ingredients for the three kinds of cookies her family members deemed essential to the celebration. She posted the recipes on her kitchen cabinet doors. When the first visitors arrived, a day or so ahead of the others, she invited them to bake the cookies. There was some surprise, perpaps a little disappointment, but it was a sugar-coated reality check that their holiday producer and director was, in fact, getting older.

Whether you are struggling to resolve an issue that affects other people or one that has consequences felt only by you, the attitude you take about the outcome can make all the difference. You've heard it before, perhaps you have heard it often, that the perfect is the enemy of the good. It's a cliché at any age but it has a special poignancy as you grow older. Because even if you can't resist aiming for perfection, you may not have the time or energy to achieve it.

So if you didn't know it before you grew old, you surely know it now: that life is all about trade-offs. Even as you adapt to some new realities, even if you make choices wisely and well, you can't have it all. That fact feels so definitive in old age.

But there are compensations. Given a wealth of life experience, there's the opportunity to make choices more knowledgeably, even as the options available are narrowing. We have a data bank about ourselves—our strengths, our vulnerabilities, our history in regard to making good and bad choices—that we can bring to bear on our decisions. We know how to prioritize, how to give more importance to some issues than others. We've confronted so many challenges over the years and refined our coping skills along the way.

## And Letting Go

There's something else to consider as you grow older. If you've always thrived on taking charge of various aspects of your life, maybe it is time to practice letting go of some of them. It's a different organizing principle, perhaps a subconscious introduction to the ultimate letting go, but offering its own rewards. Whether you seek relief, rest, or relaxation—variations on a peaceful state of being—you can learn to release some of the tension involved in maintaining control. It takes some effort if you've always understood "letting go" as an inferior attitude or a passive approach to life. In old age, it's not avoidant. It's an honorable, active choice.

Of course you want to take responsibility for yourself as long as feasible. That's a good kind of control. But you can let go—a little at a time—of taking responsibility for others. You can choose to take a back seat and let others lead. You can relinquish your tight hold on issues and agendas of all sorts. In frustrating situations, you can say to yourself, "It is what it is"—and mean it. You can ponder some questions: What's the worst thing that will happen if I skip the meeting? If I send the birthday card three days late? If I let the grass grow another inch?

Picture the scenario and see how it feels. If it's tolerable, you can try letting go of some control—becoming just a little less responsible in various endeavors.

Sharon, reluctant to tell her age but somewhere in her 70s, was the consummate volunteer. Whatever the cause, whenever the call for help, she was likely to raise her hand. She actually enjoyed the feeling of being needed, and of making a contribution. Her aging was a graceful process, not obvious to the world, with just a drop in energy level and mild arthritis in one hip. But Sharon was tired. She wanted to give up her status as the ever-ready helper, if only she could find the words to opt out when requests were made for her involvement in a project. To her amusement—and the surprise of others—she found them. When asked to participate in something that was less than compelling, she would say brightly, "Oh, I'm so sorry. I have aged out of that."

Letting go is an adventure in adaptation. Like most adventures, it takes some courage. Like most experiments, it involves some trial and error. Who knows what you will discover or how you will feel about having fewer obligations or revising your expectations of yourself? Consider it a learning experience, courtesy of aging.

# 8

## WORKING. OR NOT.

In the bygone eras of our grandparents and great-grandparents, retirement was often a fairly simple matter. You had worked long and hard. If you were lucky you were honored with a gold watch and you entered the ranks of the retired. If you had a profession or managed your own business, you might keep your hand in, seeing a few clients or acting in some advisory capacity. For many people, it was up and out.

All this has changed. As a member of a generation that is living longer and enjoying good health and vitality into old age, you may have both the time and the energy to pursue all kinds of options other than traditional retirement. That's the good news. The not-so-good reality is economic: between savings lost during a recession, ongoing threats to pensions or 401(k) plans, and the ever-increasing costs of medical treatments and long-term care, your need for income may trump any fantasy of watching old movies late into the night—with no alarm set to wake you in the morning.

Still, you may be able to withdraw from full-time employment in stages, or reinvent yourself and pursue an "encore career." Some employers have even developed "phased retirement" scenarios in which workers can notch down to part-time hours while receiving pro-rated salaries and benefits.

But if you've been a full-fledged member of the workforce and anticipate departing from it, or at least significantly revising your status, you'll need to decide when and how to proceed.

In some cases, there may be no real decision to make. Let's say you've devoted many years to an organization that has a mandatory retirement age and it's six months away. Or you've worked for an outfit with no more room to advance and there are few prospects in your field for people your age. Maybe your company offers you a buy-out and after a period of deliberation you conclude that it's too good to pass up. Maybe health issues or family responsibilities make it clear that it is time for a change.

Maybe—it happens—your job makes you miserable. Colleen is a prime example of unambivalent thinking about retirement:

> *In two hundred seventy-eight days—I'm counting them down— I'll be free to walk out the door. I've never really loved my job, but the last ten years have been the most difficult. Demanding bosses, boring assignments. But I've put in my time and contributed to my retirement funds. That feels good. Soon I will feel even better.*

If the decision to retire—let's use the word as shorthand for any significant variation on the working life in which you've been actively engaged—presents more of a dilemma, here's a process

WORKING. OR NOT.    59

to follow. Just remember that you can't be in this situation without some angst. Don't pay too much attention when some earnest friend declares that another door will open when this one closes, even if that proves true. You're not there yet.

## Facing Your Feelings

The prospect of leaving a job and relinquishing the satisfactions of a career is bound to provoke mixed emotions. Those trend to the negative if health issues of your own or the needs of people close to you or inflexible company policies dictate this change. If you loved what you did—if your work largely defined who you are—you're vulnerable to feeling sad, confused, regretful, or resentful. Or all of the above. For nearly everyone, there's ambivalence. All that time, all that energy, all those rewards—psychic and practical—and you're on the verge of giving it up.

For some people, the attachment has been to the core substance of the work itself. For others, the interpersonal relationships were primary. For still others, the prestige or the perks meant more than they might care to acknowledge. For most, it's been a mix, a potent combination of concerns, commitments, and connections.

At the deepest level, the attachment may be to life itself. It's no surprise that there's an emotional association between retirement and the end of life. This transition is a stark reminder of mortality. The determination to continue working—"let me die with my boots on"—is a metaphor for fighting to stay alive.

It doesn't help that our society tends to value performance over any other measure of our worth. That contributes to the notion of retirement as a near-death experience. Even if you find new ways to spend time and fresh uses for your ingenuity, there is still the loss of those performance-driven reinforcements of your importance—from positive reviews (evaluations and awards) to financial rewards (raises and bonuses). The suspicion that a human "doing" is superior to a human "being" rests on the fact that we are hard-wired in our Western culture to excel at the former at the expense of the latter.

Facing your feelings means making an honest appraisal of your losses. Figure out exactly what you will miss about your job or your career and how that makes you feel. Anxious, sad, fearful that you'll soon be forgotten—they're all part of your emotional inventory.

Meryl was trained as a social worker and advanced into an administrative post in her agency when she was in her 50s. Pondering the possibility of retiring next year, when she turns 65, she didn't hold back:

*Of course I know I can be a volunteer in my field. But I also know I will never again feel the excitement of presiding over a contentious staff meeting and bringing it to a successful outcome. Or seeing a child blossom as a result of my helping to make fundamental changes in a family. I may do something interesting, even meaningful, when I retire—but I know those thrills are gone.*

## Making a Decision

Once you have admitted to your own doubts and fears, consider allowing others to be part of your process. Retirement is a major life passage, whether welcomed or dreaded, and it can help to talk it out. You may want to consult with others who know you well and are able to set aside their own needs and wishes in order to help you with yours. Admit that this is a strange or difficult time for you. Invite their input as you make a two-column list of the pros and cons, benefits and costs of the decision to retire. There's no room here for anything but candor. Acknowledge reasons for staying or going that may be superficial. Include the trivial ("I like talking sports with my assistant") along with the profound ("Our sustainable energy task force is making real progress at last and I want to be part of it"). Sit with the list for a few days, go back to it, review and revise. Compare the two columns when you're satisfied that you have honestly considered all the angles of your particular situation.

Or try living in each side of your ambivalence for a period of time. For a day or even a week, pretend that you are going to continue working, just as you have been, for the foreseeable future, perhaps a year or two. When retirement thoughts intrude, let them float away and refocus on the task at hand, imagining that you will stay on in your present job. How does it feel? Are you a little disappointed or a bit relieved? Calm or anxious? Stay with it. Just take note of your mood.

Then try shifting to the other side of the ambivalence, adopting the same time frame. Pretend that you have left your work; you're in the first year or two of retirement. Naturally it will be a little harder to picture a life that you have not yet designed, but let your imagination run free. What do you feel? Apprehension or anticipation? Resentment or acceptance? A loss of control or a sense of freedom?

Denise, age 66, was all too familiar with the roller coaster of ambivalence. It helped her to name it, to give it some definition:

*I was worried about not seeing enough of my 92-year-old mother, who lived on the West Coast. And I was so tired; it felt like my biggest goal in life was to sleep later. Those two factors made me look forward to retirement with a sense of relief.*

*Then I would get back in touch with how much I loved my job. Every day there was a different intellectual problem to solve. That sort of challenge and the teamwork involved—that was cool. And I was so apprehensive about giving it up.*

> *But I was tired. After about a year of reflecting on my situation, I gave six months' notice. At the time, I said that was for the benefit of my organization, helping with the transition. But now I think the six months were really for me, to adjust, to have said it out loud. It made me think clearly, "OK, you are going to have to let go of this." I probably could have changed my mind. But I didn't.*

There's no magic here, no foolproof formula, but stay with the process, take stock of your emotions—and be open to surprises.

You might benefit from reflection of a different order, if you're still uncertain of your direction. Think back to some of the important decisions you have faced over the years. Make a list of eight or ten. Delete the ones you truly regret and any over which you still harbor misgivings. Focus exclusively on the best ones, the decisions that led to good outcomes or a solid sense of doing right by yourself, whatever the odds. Then move from that conclusion to the process itself. What do you recall about those periods of time? What resources did you use? Whom did you consult—friends, family, professionals—or did you go it alone? Did you come to a decision quickly or did you struggle, right down to the wire? Did you act on it easily, or revisit it repeatedly before you could trust it?

If you came up with a cluster of good decisions to analyze, look for any similarities in the steps you took to get to a resolution. If you note some consistency in the methods that led to positive outcomes, you may have a template—time-tested, in fact—for making a decision about retirement. If things seem more random—in one case, you never confided in anyone and in another you practically convened a village—it's still a useful exercise because you've turned up a variety of factors that you found helpful in making big decisions in the past.

Gloria made a list of eight major life decisions and was surprised—and somewhat chagrined—by what she discovered. Six of the decisions—including her choice of a college, selection of a major, and marriage at a young age—were impulsive. There was little discussion with peers and certainly no consultation with anyone who might guide or advise her. She was a solo operator and her decisions were *faits accomplis*—by the time she shared them with others, it was too late to reconsider.

Some years later, two decisions stood out in contrast. When she was divorced and the mother of teenage children, Gloria debated going to graduate school and embarking on a new career. She talked through the options with a counselor, with close friends, and with acquaintances in the field she was considering. She feels both pleasure and pride about making that significant change in her life. And when her children were grown and she no longer needed a three-bedroom house, she spent months doing research on downsizing and alternative living possibilities. She read every article containing an "empty nest" reference. She talked with everyone she knew who might offer a perspective on transforming her lifestyle. Gloria gained the confidence to move and establish a new home:

> *Based on my prior history, I think two things are important as I approach the retirement decision. The most obvious is the importance of engaging with a few other people as I try to make up my mind. It's not that they know what I should do, but the conversation makes me think about things from other angles, and more thoroughly. The other has to do with the process. I mean, it is a process. It takes time. That's very different from the way I handled some decisions that didn't turn out well, sort of all by myself sitting in a room. And not sitting there very long.*

Some of the anxiety and uncertainty surrounding the decision to retire comes from its distinctive, once-in-a-lifetime status in the array of decisions that you make over the years. "You only do it once." "There's no user manual." You are apt to come at it as though you had no preparation. In fact, you have a lifetime of decision-making to draw upon.

Decisions made in youth and middle age have a forward momentum. You choose whether to embark on a career, to enter into marriage, to have a child. To pick a vacation spot or buy a house or acquire a dog. There's a look-ahead, go-ahead aspect to these choices. In contrast, the decision to retire means looking back and letting go. It's not simple or easy and it deserves very careful consideration. At the end of the day, however, take comfort and perhaps be guided by the words of many older women and men who have made this decision: "It was time."

If you've come this far, see *Making It Happen* (Appendix II) for some practical pointers on implementing a decision to retire.

## What's Next

Do you need to know what's next? Some people's decision-making is very purposeful. They head into some version of retirement in order to have the time and energy for a specific pursuit. Or pursuits. Volunteer work, home renovation, college courses, adventure travel, hands-on grandparenting—you name it. For others, uncertainty about the future is actually liberating. The freedom to explore various options, release from responsibilities, permission to Do Nothing—these may have more appeal than making plans or setting goals for retirement.

You know who you are and what pleases you. If you were a comedian, would you prefer a script or improv? Are you temperamentally a planner or do you favor spontaneity? Do you stick to familiar routes or are you more apt to take an off-ramp without knowing where it might lead?

And whether the decision to transform your working life is highly focused or exploratory at the outset, you can always change your strategy. After all, you're the boss. Many people are surprised by the discrepancy between their original vision of life in retirement and the reality as it plays out over time, tilting in the direction of becoming less goal-oriented, less productive, more open to taking long walks and meeting friends for coffee. Sandra fits that description:

> I had been thinking about retirement from my legal career for some time, had even cut back to three days a week. But I was so afraid I would sit at home and watch soap operas, that I would become a nobody. I saw a therapist for a few months and he helped me talk about my hopes and fears. Here's the funny part. Thirty years ago, if anyone had said to me, "You're one of the ladies who lunch," I would have been indignant. Now it's one of my favorite activities, having lunch with friends.

There are exceptions, of course. Some women and men who joyfully anticipated their freedom find that they have too much time on their hands. They yearn for structure and meaning. They need to start with a practice, perhaps move on to a project. Later, we'll explore those options.

## Parting Moments

Once you have resolved your ambivalence and made a decision, don't just slip out the door. If you are saying a final goodbye to your workplace, you need to have an ending. If you are restructuring your role and your responsibilities—changing your status in any significant way—you need to mark the passage from the old to the new.

Closure matters. It's for you, so you can reflect on the past and receive whatever recognition or appreciation is offered on this occasion. And it's for your co-workers or colleagues, so they can celebrate you and congratulate you on the transition. True, there may be some thinly disguised envy in the form of bad jokes at your expense. Ignore them or laugh along with the group.

Whether because of modesty or embarrassment, many departing workers resist the idea of a retirement reception or party. Others object because it may seem insincere or pro forma. Still others resent the obligation to smile politely at the boss they never liked and make small talk with a couple of new staffers they barely know. Some, of course, welcome the attention.

Just do it. Do it because we all need rituals in our lives to measure and mark what's important. Do it because it helps to close that door so you can eventually open the next one. Do it whether you feel sad or upbeat, melancholy or cheerful. You can cry or you can laugh, or both. Just do it.

Deborah retired after 37 years as a high school teacher. She was passionate about her students and about her subject, English composition. It wasn't easy to leave what she loved, and the introvert in her was reluctant to share this momentous event with others. Still, she had participated in a monthly restaurant dinner with the other teachers in her department and felt reasonably comfortable—if hardly gregarious—in that setting. As the end of the school term approached, she told a few colleagues that this would be her ending as well. At the final dinner of the academic year, she was honored with a cake and congratulations. She was surprised, and pleased at the attendance: "Some teachers who generally looked for ways to avoid each other, who had no end of conflicts and dramas—they all came together for that dinner."

Along with agreeing to some kind of planned activity in your honor—and participating gracefully—it's important to take care of

WORKING. OR NOT. 67

any unfinished business before you depart. Is there a compliment you've always wanted to give to a long-suffering member of your team but never found the right opening? Now's the time. Are there persistent feelings of disappointment that you never expressed to your supervisor? An exit interview may give you an opening to deal with difficult issues. You'll feel better as you head down the road.

## What Comes After

If you're really leaving an organization, you will need to figure out how—and how much—to stay in touch with your workplace, if that's appealing. Maybe there are valued connections to maintain, friendships of substance beyond the work environment. It won't be the same—now you have to make arrangements to get together—but there's little doubt that these relationships have enduring value. Your ties to others and to the group as a whole are more likely to dissipate over the months and years ahead. Approaching retirement, many people like to imagine that their membership in an organization will be renewed indefinitely, despite the change in their status. They may even picture themselves as unpaid consultants or mentors. More often than not, that kind of connection diminishes over time.

Grieving—and that's what you are doing—is a long, slow process of transforming reality into memory. When you first experience any loss, it doesn't take much to provoke regression. What does that mean? In the case of retirement, regression means holding on tightly—eagerly seeking news of a project you supervised, gossip about your section members, latest developments in your field of interest. The need to belong, to identify, may remain strong. Thoughts about work and the workplace arise frequently and spontaneously. As the process of letting go evolves, your thoughts are more apt to be stimulated by particular cues—the email from a former colleague, the time of day associated with a regular departmental meeting, the sound bite on the evening news. Over time, the feelings evoked by these associations also change, losing some of their intensity.

You could even find that your work-consciousness shifts away from an active, wide-awake mode of thinking and reappears when you are sleeping. As one long-retired journalist says ruefully, "I still dream about being a reporter, imagining that I'm on a story."

Whether your departure from work takes the form of a traditional retirement or a variation on the theme, make it deliberate. Let the process unfold. Feel the feelings. Share them with others. Eventually you will achieve a kind of detachment from the work you did for so long—a detachment endowed with varying degrees of sadness or fondness, as the case may be. In the future, when you meet someone new who poses the inevitable question—"What do you do?"—you can respond with satisfaction, "I did it."

# 9

# YOUR PRACTICE, YOUR PROJECTS

Maybe you are still working, either contemplating retirement or resisting it. Perhaps you are in the process of modifying your work life in some creative fashion. Whatever your status, you'll eventually need to think about making the best use of your time and energy as you grow older. Here's where your recent adventures in self-awareness—your reflections on who you are and what matters to you—serve a purpose.

You should have a practice. You may also want a project.

## Designing a Practice

A practice is simply a pattern of behavior that is carried out time and time again. It is a routine to engage in without making lots of decisions or choices. The actions are essentially the same, over and over. At a time in life when so much is changing, think of your practice as a way to feel more stable, grounded, centered—whatever term you prefer—in the flux of advancing age.

Engaging in a practice might sound like indulging the well-known penchant of older people for what's familiar or rote, and it does trade on that sensibility. But it goes a step beyond, as an intentional and potentially satisfying way to maintain some control of your life.

If you've always worked, you already know about a practice because you had one: your job. Think of all the fixed parameters, from the hour you awoke to the time you returned home at the end of the day. In between, there were various set tasks and obligations. Even if you hadn't been employed in the traditional sense, chances are still good that you established some predictable routines in your middle years, based on the variety of responsibilities you had.

A good practice serves to give some structure to your life. As you free yourself from the constraints and dictates that shaped your earlier years, you can tailor your practice however you like. The most essential aspect is that the routine appeals to you, enough that you are willing to repeat it, over and over. As you might guess, a daily practice is desirable. Aim for developing a practice that you can carry out three times a week, at minimum.

But a good practice isn't just a dependable way to start or mark the day. It can be social or solitary, whichever you prefer. It can be as active or as contemplative as you like.

You may know right away what kind of routine would work for you. It might evolve from something that's already in place in your life. Let's say you've been going to work out at the neighborhood gym twice a week after work. Now you can add a third session and get there earlier in the day.

If nothing comes to mind, think back and wonder if there is some activity to revive or build on from your past. Maybe you enjoyed an early morning walk with a next-door neighbor until she was transferred. Maybe you started that meditation course and actually devoted five minutes daily to sitting in silence, until real life intervened. Maybe you did crossword puzzles on airplanes or while waiting for the kids at soccer practice; now you can devote thirty minutes every morning to that pleasure.

You can even construct a practice out of various elements in a combination that makes sense only to you. Grind your own coffee beans. Then take a cup of coffee to a comfortable spot and read the entire sports section of the newspaper, including some sports you never used to follow. Or brew tea, head to that favorite chair, listen to classical music, and take up your knitting for forty-five minutes.

You may want to analyze your days or weeks in terms of what's missing from your life—or if you're still employed, will someday be missing. If it's the pleasure of conversation with co-workers, your practice needs to include the companionship of others. If it's physical activity, make sure your practice involves movement in some form, from restorative to vigorous. If advancing age has you nervous about gradually losing your mind—has anyone been spared that worry?—choose a practice that engages your brain.

It's important that your practice be essentially unproductive. There may be an outcome—you finished the puzzle—but there's nothing *produced*. Because the moment you think productively, you leave the realm of the predictable and the familiar. We're after sameness here. You'll still have time in the day and energy left over for the stimulation of a project, which meets different needs.

A practice is somewhat similar to a hobby, the enjoyable leisure time activity that you were supposed to fit in between your hours at work and hours spent on other obligations, back in the day. With one key difference—you want to keep the emphasis on the process rather than the outcome.

Georgia, age 72, is a professional musician who has played the flute since she was very young, but always with an eye to the next audition or concert performance. In retirement, she developed a daily practice that was limited to pieces she knew well and loved, a kind of musical indulgence to start her day.

Karen, age 67, recently retired as a medical records specialist, a job involving long commutes to and from work. She mentioned two conditions for a practice: that she could do it without leaving home and that she would find it calming. Her first foray has been to spend twenty minutes each morning drinking her coffee and working on a jigsaw puzzle, an activity she has always enjoyed.

Mark and Jeffrey, both in their 70s, met many years ago in their local running club. Mark continues to enjoy good health but Jeffrey is coping with the consequences of a diagnosis of Lyme disease. After attending some stretch-and-balance classes at their gym, they designed a daily home practice based on the same poses and moves—with an occasional gentle exercise video from YouTube for variety. Late morning works best for Jeffrey.

Lee continues to take pleasure from a practice he designed when he first retired, ten years ago. In his ritual, which takes a little over a half hour, he makes breakfast. Some elements are constant: brewing the coffee, setting his place, pouring the juice, toasting the toast to just the right degree, selecting the jam. One will always be a work in progress: achieving the perfect fried egg. He actually enjoys the clean-up, completing a succession of orderly tasks while listening to a podcast.

It doesn't matter how long it takes to practice your practice. Fifteen minutes may suffice if you choose something meditative or cerebral or domestic. You'll need more time if you go to a yoga class or head to the driving range. Or make Lee's breakfast.

Be sure to label your practice as your practice, whether you are talking to yourself or mentioning it to someone else. Calling something by a name makes it more real, and you'll be more apt to implement your plan. Telling another person what you have in mind also improves the odds that you will follow through on your intention.

After a while, you can tweak your practice, even abandon it and find another. But it's a good idea to have a serious trial run before making those changes.

When you come up with an idea, imagine doing it, practicing it over time—one week, two months, maybe a year from now. If that image appeals—or even if you are simply curious—just begin.

In the relatively unscripted, unscheduled days of old age, your practice serves as a buffer against waking up and having little or no sense of what to do next. Some people find that it is enough to sustain them, along with the ordinary business of maintenance—be it taking care of the body or the home, along with financial or family responsibilities. They feel stable and secure. Toss in some entertainment, perhaps add some travel, and they relish the freedom from time pressures and the other demands of their younger years.

## Choosing a Project

But for many people, even a well-conceived and reliable practice is not enough to satisfy their interests or their wish to matter or make a difference in the world. They want something more dynamic and goal-oriented: a project.

The hallmarks of a project are creativity, expansion, productivity—qualities that activate the imagination, deepen knowledge, facilitate accomplishment. Many people give top priority to a project that serves the needs of others.

Remember your first résumé with the line at the top where you described your ideal job? The definition of your project is the old-age equivalent. It may play on some talents that you already

## 74    YOUR PRACTICE, YOUR PROJECTS

possess but put to a different use. It may be a matter of combining your existing skill set with gaining new knowledge. Or it could be a completely new venture, the kind where people who know you react in surprise—and no small amount of envy—when they hear what you're doing.

Parents and school teachers are familiar with the notion that in order to thrive, children need both roots and wings. The same can be said of older people. If a practice can root you, a project can give you wings: the chance to learn something new, the freedom to create in whatever medium you choose, the opportunity to tackle a challenge of any sort.

Your project can be stimulating or merely engrossing. And while your supply of energy (and your wallet) may put some limits on your ambitions, you are protected in any endeavor by a no-fault clause. You can "fail" and move on. Any project in old age, however serious or frivolous, is an experiment in determining what suits your time and talent and inclinations. You don't have to get it right the first time. You don't have to get it right at all.

Imagine some of the possibilities. There's the learning category: auditing college courses, brushing up on a second language, attending a lecture series, studying genealogy. The good works category: volunteer service of all kinds. The career-extended category: part-time worker, consultant, mentor. The arts and crafts category, the sports category, the cooking category. In all of these, the choices are similar. You can opt to refine or enhance the skills you already possess.

Or you can dare to try something new. If, for example, you've been doubtful but curious about the ways modern technology might enhance your old age, there's a lot to explore.

Julia, just shy of her 79th birthday, was coping with progressive loss of her eyesight. A friend encouraged her to buy a tablet that would allow her to magnify pages, as needed. The same friend

## YOUR PRACTICE, YOUR PROJECTS

kindly offered tech support as Julia learned how to use the device. Her project has made it possible for her to read the novels she loves.

Daniel is an octogenarian who proudly lives independently, but no longer drives. His daughter-in-law Elisa offered to drive him to his medical appointments and to his visits with family and friends. He appreciated her offer but claimed he didn't want to be that dependent on her. When she suggested that he use a ride service, he objected to the expense—until she asked him to compare the cost of these occasional expeditions with the annual upkeep of his own car in the past. It took a bit longer for Daniel to admit to the real obstacle: his unfamiliarity with the ride service app on the smartphone his family had insisted he purchase a few years ago "for his safety." They made it into a project, Elisa coaching him until he was an app expert.

Arthur is reluctant to reveal his age, but I'm guessing he's in his late 60s. He's tech-savvy, perfectly conversant with all kinds of devices and platforms. As a widower nearing retirement, he's quite aware of his potential for loneliness once he leaves the world of work. So his project is to carefully research his options for reaching out, staying connected through social media or meet up groups. Some friends have even suggested online dating. He's cautious, but willing to explore.

You may wonder how choosing a project in old age differs from signing up for any of the activities you've engaged in over the years. It's probably more deliberate—you're bringing that lifetime of experience to the process—and there's a matter of emphasis, of making it your own.

For example, time was when your best friend could pressure you into spending some of your Saturday afternoons helping out with his favorite charity. Or perhaps your own idealism or sense of obligation propelled you into things you just didn't enjoy. Now

# YOUR PRACTICE, YOUR PROJECTS

that time is finite, spend that limited resource on things that truly appeal to you.

Then take the matter of responsibility. When we're younger, we're apt to be eager for responsibility. That's where satisfaction, not to mention authority, lies. In old age, you need to think carefully—do I have the energy or the endurance to shoulder the demands of this particular project? Do I have the resilience to deal with the inevitable frustrations and disappointments that go with a leadership role? Maybe yes. But don't be afraid to say no.

Think about reclaiming a project from your past. Travel your own memory lane and see what you discover. It could be a hobby you discarded, designing electric train layouts or baking bread. Or a dream you deferred—perhaps improving your Spanish or finishing *War and Peace*.

Or something entirely different.

Ellen, about to turn 70, wanted to volunteer for a worthy cause. Initially, she imagined a project that would be global in context, or at least national in its implications. Imagine her surprise at learning about a group of older citizens in her city neighborhood who pick up litter. Equipped with trash bags and lifter tongs, they head out together for an hour or so every morning, scanning the sidewalks in search of cigarette butts, soda cans, and discarded carry-out containers. Sometimes they chat a bit, sometimes not. Ellen loves this very local project.

Also consider that you have old-person privilege to pursue a project of enduring significance, a legacy. You can write your own memoir. You can scan family photographs, assemble memorabilia from generations past. You can create an audio or video history by interviewing other family members—making sure that someone interviews you. You can research and document the history of your town or your neighborhood or any other subject of abiding interest to you. These are all opportunities to make a record of your own

## YOUR PRACTICE, YOUR PROJECTS

life in the context of people, places, or things that matter to you, a record that will live on after you are gone. A bid for immortality? Why not?

When you are older, time and energy are not the renewable resources that they once were. If you don't have forever (and some of your time is reserved for naps) it only makes sense to choose your ventures wisely. Invest yourself—perhaps with the same degree of determination or enthusiasm you have always mustered—but invest selectively.

It's appealing, this notion of choice. But it may be a luxury you can ill afford in your later years if you bear responsibility for the care of others. A spouse with a disabling condition. Grandchildren in need of supervision. A close friend with no surviving family members. If your life is defined by this kind of commitment, consider it your project. It's dynamic because it's ever-changing and involves the creative use of a wide variety of skills and aptitudes. It's goal-oriented by definition: your purpose is to improve the quality of life of someone you love. The entertainment quotient may be low—we're not really looking for fun here—but the sense that what you do matters, that you are making a difference, is profound. Keep in mind, however, that you can't keep giving out unless you get something back in. Think about finding some way to restore yourself. Talk to others living similar lives, whether you find them at a support group or the neighborhood bar. Try not to go it alone.

There's one more project to contemplate. Taking care of yourself. It's not so simple in old age. The tasks of routine maintenance multiply. Health issues become more complex. Energy diminishes and memory declines. To remain as independent as possible, it may well be that most—possibly all—of your physical and emotional resources need to be devoted to the project of self-care.

This responsibility—taking care of yourself in old age—is self-centered in the best possible way. It can give you a sense of accomplishment and reinforce your independence. You're still in charge, to the best of your abilities. It's safe to say you probably never imagined that carrying out the activities of daily living was anything notable, let alone impressive. You took it for granted that you brushed your teeth, fixed breakfast, took your vitamins. Now, as you grow older, the minor and menial details of life become more prominent. They constitute your infrastructure and they deserve your attention. And respect. Take some satisfaction from accomplishing them.

## Why This Matters

What are we after here, with these notions of a practice and a project? Why not simply wing it through old age? After a lifetime spent making plans and keeping to a schedule, surely you deserve to invent each day as you go along, if that's what appeals. An endless vacation. Sort of.

But there's a universal need for structure in our lives that we can't afford to ignore. Whether you welcome it or resent it, structure is essential. We all thrive by having some order in our daily life as a buttress against the confusion of the world around us. Think back again to early childhood. Even the most relaxed parents provide some organization for their small child. Eating and sleeping may be loosely regulated but they aren't entirely haphazard. As time goes on, more strictures are added until the child acquires membership in a complex network of customs and rules to live by. In old age—here's the good part—you can shed some of those expectations or revise the governing principles. You can organize your days and weeks to suit yourself. But the need for at least a modicum of structure persists, and you do well to honor it.

Whether you are developing a practice or pursuing a project, these initiatives serve another vital purpose. They represent maintaining some control of your life at the very time that so much—let's face it—is beyond your control. The vicissitudes of health, the vagaries of family life, the very complexity of the geopolitical and socioeconomic worlds we live in—how much power do you actually have to influence these spheres? It makes good sense to make your small corner of the universe as pleasing or satisfying as possible, within the limits of your circumstances. You know who you are and what you care about. You can be deliberate in channeling your emotions, allocating your energy, directing your behavior. Older, wiser.

# 10

## MOVING. OR NOT.

On any list of life's Top Ten Stressful Events, making a move to a new location ranks high. Does anyone ever exclaim with delight, "Here comes the moving van!"? Not likely. An absence of enthusiasm is understandable, given the combination of difficult decision-making and the complicated logistics involved in relocating yourself (and possibly other people), as well as furniture, plants, and pets.

All moves share some common characteristics, but a move in later life is endowed with its own distinctive qualities. It's harder to manage the physical demands of a move when your strength is a bit compromised or your energy flags by mid-afternoon; it's not

## MOVING. OR NOT.

easy to stay on top of the details if your best multi-tasking days are behind you.

When you were younger, you could settle somewhere for a few months—even years—and conclude, "I'm not loving this." It may have been relatively easy, when you were quite mobile and your requirements somewhat flexible, to move on. As you grow older, there are more constraints, some practical and some emotional. If you've lived in one place for a long time, it's all that much harder to leave it behind. Most profoundly, there is a feeling—a fear—that a particular move could be the last one you make, to the last place you live on this planet. It takes courage to face that possibility.

But unless you are a true nomad, you need a home. And here's an opportunity to bring your self-awareness into play, coupled with constructive research into the various options for living comfortably as you grow older. Knowing yourself so well allows you to judge the alternatives against your own needs and wishes; your research gives you vital information about the possibilities. Add to this mix a candid appraisal of your current physical condition, along with any projection you are able to make about your health in the future. A reasonable formula for that prediction might involve two parts realism—based on your here-and-now data—and one part hope.

Many—perhaps most—older women and men would prefer to "age in place," staying in their familiar home environment as long as possible. In other cultures and eras, this was the norm. Your family or your tribe or your village was committed to sheltering and caring for its older generation. In the Western world in the 21st century, not so much.

You can age in place, wherever you desire, if you have the financial resources to maintain your home and hire the help you may need in the coming years. Absent such riches, you can age in place if you are endowed with a different kind of wealth—a family with enough members, energy, and commitment to support you when

MOVING. OR NOT. 83

you need it. And you may be able to stay where you are if your community sponsors one of the burgeoning organizations whose mission is to facilitate aging in place with the help of volunteer networks. Or if you're willing to consider sharing your space with a housemate or roommate. Arrangements can vary from the simple expedient of dividing expenses and chores to an exchange that involves caregiving responsibilities.

One variation on aging in place involves moving from your present living situation and downsizing to smaller quarters in the same city or town, hoping to live out your years in a more compact new home. You'll probably have to face parting company with some of your possessions, which is no small feat. (We'll look at how to do it in the next chapter.) You'll need to say goodbye to neighbors; you may stay in touch but it won't be the same. You'll need to let go of your fond associations to a particular tree or view from a kitchen window. You'll be bringing closure to the history made in that place.

The plot thickens, if you consider moving to an entirely new locale. You'll want to pay attention to all the relevant trade-offs. The known versus the somewhat-unknown or just-plain-unknown. The loss of a familiar environment versus the adventure of someplace new. Separation from friends and acquaintances versus the opportunity to make new connections.

You'll need to do more research if the prospect of a retirement home or continuing care retirement community has any appeal. You'll want to read up on the different levels of care offered in these institutions, the entrance requirements, and the financial arrangements. If at all possible, make an in-person visit; some retirement communities offer an overnight stay as a way for you to meet residents and scope out the territory.

Again, the trade-offs. Contemplate the loss of complete control over your living situation versus being dependent on others.

## MOVING. OR NOT.

Autonomy versus collaboration. Freedom versus security. Of course the contrasts aren't quite so stark, but you get the idea.

A word about other influences. Grown children head the list. They are often the catalysts for moving you to a haven, typically some sort of congregate living facility near them that they think of as safer or more secure than your current home. You may concur, or at least be willing to accede to their wishes if it spares them some anxiety over your welfare. Close friends may exert pressure as well. Perhaps they are optimistically headed to some sort of supported living venue themselves, or they picture such places as highly undesirable. It's like the decision to retire: listen all you want, but be guided by your own instincts.

If you are favored with good health and adequate energy, you can choose another way to live closer to your offspring by establishing your own home not far away from them. This option offers the potential for more daily involvement and caretaking, as needed. But there are important issues to consider. Can you count on your grown child (or children) not to relocate, once you have moved to be closer? How much time together do you both anticipate? How do your other adult children feel about your proximity to the chosen one? What role do you want to play with grandchildren? Whatever your concerns, a frank exchange about expectations will improve the odds that this scenario will end up serving the best interests of all involved.

### No Simple Chart

There's no simple chart to help you make this decision, but there are a few cautions to keep in mind.

First, identify the pluses and minuses, pros and cons, to making any change in your living situation. That old standby, the two-column list, is useful here. Even if you're not a habitual list-maker,

MOVING. OR NOT. 85

make one now, with "make a move" on one side and "stay put" on the other. Draw a horizontal line through each column, in the middle of the page. Above the line, enter the benefits of each option; below the line note the downsides. Rather than adding up to some kind of score, the goal is to use your imagination and anticipate all of the variables as best you can.

Christopher, a 79-year old widower, was thinking about relocating as his upcoming milestone birthday approached. Under the "make a move" heading, he wrote some potential benefits: a fresh start after his recent loss, freedom from the never-ending demands of repairs and maintenance that his older home required, the possibility of more walking and less driving if he found the right neighborhood. On the downside, apart from the obvious effort of relocation, he faced the reality of that fresh start: that he would give up the familiarity and the treasured associations to his late wife that his present home represented.

When he listed reasons to "stay put," the emotional attachment to his current surroundings ranked high as a benefit. On the other hand, he could imagine the downside. He could picture himself in a kind of limbo, not reaching out to connect socially or involve himself in new activities.

Christopher's conclusion was to wait another year before making this decision. He saw the value of taking this approach to his dilemma, to gain more clarity about both sides of the issue. In particular, he is motivated to make use of the insight about living alone. He is actively looking for times and places to interact with other people, a hedge against loneliness.

Annette and Roland, both in their early 70s, are a classic example of a couple who disagree about moving. Or not. Annette is determined to take what she views as a last chance to furnish and decorate a home in a style that pleases her. Roland, a creature of habit by his own admission, can't imagine altering his domestic patterns no matter how lovely the surroundings—he knows where the coffee is stored in the kitchen, how carefully the dishwasher must be loaded to avoid mishap, where his keys are kept by the front door. And it's not all about Roland. He firmly believes that their aging dog Lola will also suffer from any change in routine.

Neither partner was enthusiastic about making a list of their concerns, but they were willing to do it. Annette initially balked at coming up with any benefit to "staying put," but she acknowledged the value of continuing to live in the house that her two grandchildren thought of as their second home. Plus, she could consider a bathroom renovation that would be aging-appropriate, and various other upgrades to satisfy her inner interior designer. Roland was similarly resistant to finding anything positive about "making a move," unless they found something close to their offspring, with much less grass to mow.

The couple is continuing the conversation as they search real estate listings on the internet. They are making progress. Roland no longer sighs heavily at the mere mention of moving. For the first time, Annette has accepted—without criticizing—the reasons for his reluctance. If they make a move, she vows to be actively involved in helping Roland re-establish his routines, especially those that include Lola.

If you are inclined to relocate, you might think of it as trading in one batch of nuisances or frustrations for another, rather than fantasizing that you're headed to heaven on earth. There may be some obvious gains—such as no more snow shoveling in warmer climes. You could be so tired of the devil you know that you're willing to take a chance on the one you don't know. Your finances or your health—or both—may make a persuasive argument in favor of change. But there's also a good chance that the decision will not be doubt-free. It makes sense to recognize that. Besides, with your lifetime of experience, you can handle it.

A word about that lifetime. Over the years, you've accumulated all kinds of imagery about old people and their environments, much of it negative. You can do a slide show in your mind of your frail great-aunt alone in the deteriorating apartment she wouldn't leave, and that never-forgotten visit to a nursing home where there were bad smells in the hallways. We all have a store of these impressions, which can't be excised but need to be taken for what they are: understandable reactions of your youthful self confronting some shocking aspects of aging in undesirable conditions.

At any age, a variety of prejudices can interfere in the process of figuring out how to live as you grow older. They are all different versions of an internalized bias against aging. You'll want to review your own. Maybe you sympathize with Madelyn. Recovering from a minor stroke at age 85, she withdrew her application to move to a retirement home because she saw "too many residents on walkers" when she went for an interview. Or with Daniel, who—as you may remember from the previous chapter—received a kind offer from his daughter-in-law Elisa to drive him to his doctors' appointments. Initially he rejected her offer in an understandable but misguided effort to assert his independence as long as possible. Madelyn and Daniel had this in common: neither wanted to identify themselves as "old," despite the evidence. They were determined to maintain their denial, ignoring the risks to their health and well-being.

When facing the decision to move-or-not-move, you'll want to examine your preconceptions in order to minimize their influence over your problem-solving. Even if your instinct is to hold them fast, now is the time to rethink any overly sentimental or patently unrealistic beliefs: "I refuse to live someplace where everyone is the same age," "I've always enjoyed good health and I don't see why that would change," "It's too hard to make new friends," "I can't stand the thought of some stranger living in my house." These are common examples of self-defeating attitudes. You may want to add one of your own.

Another resource for your decision-making involves reviewing the relocations in your past. There's likely to be relevant material. In addition to recalling the specifics—where and when—how did you feel? What helped you make the move, emotionally or logistically? How did you adjust afterward? How would you arrange a relocation differently, if you decide to do it again?

Timing matters. If you've started to think about making a move, keep thinking. You need some lead time to do your research and check out the options against your own priorities. You need even more time if you are selling and/or buying property, in the locale where you live or somewhere new. If a retirement community is your destination, add in some waiting time for a desirable unit to become available.

Most important, you're getting older, Make the change while you still have the capacity to manage various challenges. Physically, it's hard to let go of that image of your youthful self packing heavy boxes and hoisting them effortlessly, then driving an overloaded van hundreds of miles to the new location, all in 24 hours. Respect your older body and its limits. You'll also need the adaptability to handle the logistics. If your heart and mind are open to new experiences, so much the better.

## Coming Full Circle

You are coming full circle. When you were a baby, your immediate world was very small—but it was big enough for you. You were warm and snug. As you grew, you left your cocoon and went forth to explore. Making a home was less compelling than having a life. Perhaps you stuffed all of your belongings in a backpack and hit the open road. As you grew older, your priorities shifted, and you

MOVING. OR NOT.    89

settled down. Soon you needed a home, a home big enough to hold people and possessions. Maybe you expanded even further— more bedrooms, a bigger backyard.

Now you're moving in the other direction. You may be wide-ranging in your interests and global in your outlook and that's admirable. But you don't need to occupy as much of the planet as you once thought you did. For some people, simplicity itself is a value, and they enjoy edging closer to that ideal. For others, it's more a matter of casting off some of the responsibility for home maintenance and management. What was once attractive or seemed necessary in terms of scope and scale has lost its charm.

Think about what you actually need in terms of physical space and what seems essential in your surroundings. Maybe that's an argument for staying in place. If it's not, identify the alternatives and choose what's best—"best" as shorthand for appealing and realistic in reasonable proportions—for you.

Be aware that significant grieving is likely to accompany the process of making a change in where you live. It's not unlike the retirement decision, when you depart from a familiar space and place. It's similar in that you need to make the change in your life explicit, by calling up the memories, naming the losses, sharing your ambivalent feelings with people who will listen sympathetically.

Even if you've taken dozens of photographs in your home, now's the time to take more. Focus this album on the place and its surroundings, the interior and the exterior. Think about Marjorie and Sam, an older couple in their late 70s who treasured the dining room cabinets they designed and installed themselves, decades earlier. Several years after leaving that home, they still look at their pictures of those cabinets with a little sadness and a great deal of pride. Which especially comfortable corner or pleasing arrangement on a built-in bookshelf would you most like to document? Maybe, ruefully, that dent in the wall that never got repaired? Of course you'll take a photo of the door frame if it has pencil marks charting the heights of children or grandchildren as they grew up.

In another parallel to departure from a workplace, consider some kind of farewell to this home, recognizing the good times—and, perhaps, the not so good—with people who have shared in your history there. It can be a simple gathering for morning coffee or something more lavish and celebratory. The point is to mark the occasion of the ending of your tenure in that place. By honoring your attachment to your old home, you open the door to living well in the next one.

If you expect to stay where you are, you can shift your focus to planning sensible modifications of your living quarters. Grab bars in the shower, good task lighting, functional smoke detectors, important phone numbers easily available. Consider signing up for a medical alert system that notifies the fire department or someone you designate in case of emergency.

Moving or not moving, make the decision deliberately and develop a plan to implement it, task by task. Let yourself admit to the feelings that go with this life transition, your own emotional mixture of apprehension and anticipation. Trust your own instincts and abilities, and ask for help when you need it. It's a puzzle with many parts, this question of where to live as you advance in years. But you can bring your self-awareness and life experience to bear on solving it. Older, wiser.

# 11

## LIGHTEN UP

Household items … clothes … sports equipment … collections of all kinds. As you've grown older, have you occasionally felt burdened by the sheer number of objects in your possession? Tired of keeping track of them or dusting them or wondering how to arrange them or store them? If so, you may be the ideal candidate for lightening up, a slow but steady effort to say good-bye to some of your worldly goods.

The project may be intimidating—it's hard work—but you can imagine the reward. You're almost ready to edit your holdings, distributing some things around the world and just plain disposing of others. You look forward to the simplicity of caring for fewer things. As Susan, approaching her 70th birthday, explained it, "I feel

LIGHTEN UP

like I'm living in a museum to my past. This museum needs a curator, someone to deaccession a few of the holdings. I guess it's me."

But for so many older people, this prospect is hard to envision, let alone attempt. They might prefer to identify with the ancient Egyptians who filled their tombs with all kinds of beloved objects, along with food and drink for the afterlife. No need for them to downsize. But in this life, if you anticipate a move from a house to an apartment or a retirement community, or cohabitation with a relative or friend, your space will shrink. Put simply, your stuff won't fit.

Theodore and Anna, now in their late 50s, entered the Foreign Service when they were only in their 20s. After dozens of relocations around the world, they know how to do it well. When asked if they had any advice for older people facing moves, here's Ted's response:

> *Our approach works for folks of any age. It's not so much about the packing, but about the unpacking. Ask yourself, "How will I feel when I unwrap this object in my new space?" If you anticipate greeting an old friend, the item qualifies for the move. If you groan inwardly and wonder why you dragged a dozen empty jam jars—you gave up canning long ago—to a new destination, give yourself permission to bid them goodbye.*

Of course it's a challenge when you care deeply about many of the items in your personal inventory, whether they are a testament to the hard work that earned them or to the good taste that acquired them or to the relationship that provided them. They're a security blanket. It's natural to want to hold on to what you've accumulated. The prospect of loosening your grip makes you anxious. It feels like letting go of the life you've led, in bits and pieces. Parting with books ... outgrown children's toys ... a Monopoly game with missing pieces ... your grandparents' National Geographic magazines ... and that crockpot you bought but never used.

LIGHTEN UP     93

A word about that security blanket. You may be someone who feels most confident and content when surrounded by many objects in your personal space. You don't mind what others might call clutter. In fact, the sheer number of things and their crowded disarray feels normal to you. If you're motivated—for any reason—to rearrange and edit and part with some of these possessions, that's fine. If your storehouse of goods poses any hazard to your health or risk to your well-being, even better. But keep in mind that only positive reinforcement is helpful when we attempt to change the status quo of our collections, our stash of things. Negative labels—"pack rat" or "hoarder"—inhibit our momentum when we're facing a challenge with this degree of emotional difficulty. We need our efforts recognized, some affirmation that we're making progress, one box or drawer at a time. If no one else can deliver that message, be sure to deliver it yourself.

It's possible that the prospect of a less-encumbered life is intriguing to you. More likely, it is fast becoming desirable and even a necessity as you grow older. In either case, let's take a look at the practical process of lightening up.

You're not going to make any big decisions, not yet. But you do have to start by choosing your first category—books, kitchen items, clothes, tools, whatever—for thoughtful consideration. Gather as many of these related items as you wish and assemble them in one place. Depending on the size of your inventory, it could be a table or a floor where there's not much foot traffic. Once you select your space, you'll need to find a way to divide it into three sections. Then create a label for each one: *Discards, Find New Homes,* and *Keep No Matter What.* After you tape or prop up these signs in your staging area, take a break.

In the next phase, you ponder the future of your possessions and place them, one by one, in the most appropriate section. Maybe you're looking at something that has outlived its useful life—might it be eligible for the *Discards* pile? Sometimes a worn-out T-shirt is destined to be a rag or a badly chipped mug deserves to be tossed. But not without honor.

Reflect for a moment and thank the object—however silly that may seem—for its service to you over the years. Thanks to the silk-screened shirt our high school class wore at our 25th reunion! Thanks for all those 6 a.m. cups of coffee! This ritual of expressing gratitude applies whenever you intend to part company with an object, not just the relatively few things that are headed to the trash. It's a little bit of life review, pausing to remember the people or place or circumstance with which the item is associated. Say it out loud, softly if you wish: Thank you.

Roger had collected baseball caps for many years. They didn't take up a lot of room and he figured he could store them on the top shelf of one of the closets in the retirement home to which he would move in a few months. He reconsidered:

*I got to thinking. For one thing, I knew I wasn't going to be able to reach that shelf easily. So they would sit there. I decided to spend time with each one and then figure out what to do. Great baseball memories! Like the games I went to with my father when I was a boy. The team my best friend and I rooted for despite their losing performance, season after season, until we gave up. And there's our city's winning team right now, I'm such a fan, I have three of their caps in different colors.*

*I chose two favorites to go with me in my move. I put the rest in a bag. This spring I am going to take them to the Little League practice near me and see if those kids would have fun with them.*

Let's develop some guidelines for this project. You could set a timer for 30 minutes. You could set a quota for the day, promising to deal with five objects and renewing that commitment each day

LIGHTEN UP    95

until you are done. The main point is to give this enterprise some structure. The variations are for you to design.

Assembling and sorting and determining the future of your personal belongings isn't easy work, so feel free to experiment. Maybe 30 minutes is too much and you need to keep it to 15. Maybe the daily quota should be a minimum of three items and a maximum of five.

Keep in mind that this effort is emotionally stressful. Be kind to yourself. It's much better to proceed slowly rather than trying to plow through, only to find that you can't sustain the pace and that you and your possessions have arrived at an unfriendly impasse.

Now let's tackle the more complicated choices. Most of us live life surrounded by things in perfectly good condition. We just don't really need them. And we don't always have room for them as we grow older, whether that's psychological or practical. We need to *Find New Homes* for them.

Home-finding is really recycling, although not in the original sense of composting or repurposing or providing the raw material for some new industrial use. This is personal recycling in which we have an opportunity to choose the new owner of something we've cared about.

After reflecting on—and honoring—your past association or history with an object, focus on selecting someone who would make good use of it or simply enjoy it. Finding the framed poster a new home is just as worthwhile as keeping it out of the landfill.

If you have friends or family members who might appreciate some of your belongings, start on the process of passing things around. You may feel a sense of satisfaction, albeit poignant, when a beloved possession finds a new life in a younger person's home. Fred and Dorothea, both in their late 60s, bypassed their nephew's online wedding registry and offered the bride and groom a favorite piece from their pottery collection:

96    LIGHTEN UP

*It was a little hard to let go of that bowl we bought years ago on a trip to California. We actually used it as a mixing bowl when we didn't have much kitchen equipment. It survived that phase, and later we gave it more status as a salad bowl when we had company over. When we wrapped it up, we included a note to Kevin and his fiancée, explaining all of this. They sent us a sweet reply, said they hoped we would come for dinner after the wedding and see it on their table.*

Many older people have more objects to deaccession than they have family, friends, or acquaintances. You can sell things on eBay or Craig's List. You can give things away to organizations that sponsor thrift shops or distribute household objects to people in need. You can donate things to charity events. Books can go to the local library book sale. If you're lucky enough to live in a locale that sponsors freecycling, you can post a notice online that your still-in-good-condition camping equipment is available and then choose the lucky recipient from among the many eager responses. No money changes hands, just good will.

*Keep No Matter What* sounds obvious—these are the belongings you can't bear to part with. If you have room in your life for all of them, how fortunate! You've taken a good look at the stuff-of-many-decades and selected what really matters to you; you have the space to arrange or store them.

If you're not that fortunate, proceed with caution. Take as much time as possible to reconsider the status of any apple-of-your-eye object. Recall how much it has meant to you, possibly for many years. Reconstruct the memories it holds, whether it reminds you of your favorite high school teacher or your first love or that big promotion. And if circumstances eventually require that you find the object a new home, take a photo of it before you part company. That image—and your memories—are yours to keep.

If all of this seems overwhelming, consider enlisting a companion in the process. It may feel better to have someone else around as you make these decisions about things that have so much meaning for you. If you're unwilling to draft a helper, or if it's impractical, at least turn on the TV or play some good music for company while you work.

After she retired from her career as a tax accountant, Rachel, age 67, thought about moving. She wanted to live closer to her sister, find new activities, and enjoy a warmer climate. She had plenty of available time and energy; the financial aspects of settling in the new location were favorable. But there was no way she could put her townhouse on the market in its present condition. The basement was filled with items she had stored, not only the china and keepsakes she had inherited from her parents, but also the boxes she had never completely unpacked from her last move ten years ago.

Rachel was familiar with the provocative approach to decluttering in which you take stock of your belongings and discard anything that fails to make you feel joyful. She envied people for whom that might be effective, but knew she needed a different strategy. She succeeded at the first step, marking her staging area. At that point she faltered. She balked at the thought of dragging the heavy boxes upstairs by herself; she also realized that the scope of the project—a lonely enterprise—was greater than previously imagined.

Rachel knew a high school student who mowed lawns in the summer. He was eager to earn some extra money and in a few hours made short work of lifting and transporting the boxes upstairs. Thinking of someone to keep her company and encourage her wasn't as easy, until she remembered two co-workers who said how much they would miss her and urged her to keep in touch after the retirement party:

*I wasn't sure that helping me downsize was what they had in mind, but I reached out. Their response was positive, and the two of them took turns on Saturday afternoons over the next two months. We shared work gossip first and then they let me go back to my tasks. One helper turned on the TV to watch football; the other used the time to catch up on email. I didn't need assistance with the specifics of my project, but I was extremely grateful for the presence of other people. I felt less alone.*

The decision-making—whether it takes hours, days, or weeks—is the hardest part of lightening up. Now you can shift gears and focus on the disposal of the Discards and the implementation of Fine New Homes. Timing is important.

With the Discards, be decisive. Put those items in the trash or the recycling bin or whatever option your community provides. Keep in mind that you've already thought this through; no need to go back to Square One after such deliberate consideration.

With the Find New Homes, give yourself some leeway to track down the appropriate recipients, be they individuals or organizations, and time to arrange or make the delivery—but not so much time that you waffle and slip the items back into your closet. Roger put those baseball caps in a bag marked To Little League Next April so he wouldn't forget his plan. Rachel decided to contribute some of her parents' household goods to an agency sponsoring halfway houses for women newly released from prison. One of her former workmates offered to help, and they made a date for the drop-off.

When you've done a good job—which is to say thorough—with one category, give yourself credit. It's well deserved, even if this effort is not the kind of accomplishment that the world is apt to recognize, let alone applaud. Then move on to the next category, those half-empty paint cans or holiday decorations.

As always, remember to say goodbye. Express your appreciation to your worldly goods and wish them well in their next life— whatever and wherever that may be.

# 12

## DO LESS. BE MORE.

Let's pause here and revive that old joke about the human "doing" versus the human "being." Aging brings this distinction into focus. Our circumstances—inner and outer—gradually dictate a shift away from the sometimes frenetic activity, the busyness, of youth and middle age.

You may think of this transition as a loss, or perhaps a cavalcade of losses. You're not hitting the ground running; you may not even feel like getting out of bed first thing in the morning. Your calendar isn't chock-a-block with notes on where you need to be or what you need to do; your commitments are fewer and farther between. Your adrenalin isn't pumping with the old intensity; no need to raise your blood pressure when there's ample time for whatever the day brings. There's an obvious risk inherent in these changes, that you interpret this new mode as your failure to measure up to an old standard of achievement. You may feel it as a kind of passivity, laced with disappointment.

The reality is that you've lived long enough to explore your state of being, even if you've never been much for introspection—let alone contemplation. Now you're given an opportunity. Back in the day, some of us were captivated by the exhortation to "trust the process." Maybe you're finally ready to go down paths where the outcome is uncertain or unimportant, where the journey itself is the reward. It's still your "one wild and precious life," as the poet Mary Oliver tells us; only the nature of the possibilities has been transformed.

Contemplation sounds so simple, as the dictionary defines it: "to think profoundly and at length." And yet it was so elusive—or difficult, bordering on impossible—for many of us when we were younger. The good news is that old age is the perfect time to revisit the possibility of contemplation. You could even say that contemplation is the special province and privilege of old age.

For one thing, you have the time for it. On a daily basis, you probably have more time as you withdraw from managing multiple demands and responsibilities and begin to simplify your life, at least a little. Life experience is relevant, too. You can reminisce selectively, recalling the best times, replaying scenes from long ago. Nostalgia has a bad reputation as sentimental indulgence when it is really a wistful appreciation of your past. Mortality may play a part, too, if you face the eventual ending of life as you know it and are inclined to ponder what may or may not lie beyond. Taken together, these elements create the right circumstances for late-in-life reflection.

Breath is another dimension that deserves attention as you grow older. For much of our lives, we took our breathing for granted, inhaling and exhaling without giving it much, if any, thought. Unless you had a medical condition that affected your respiration, or performed as a concert singer, or monitored your lung capacity as an elite athlete, you didn't pay much attention to the constant in-and-out of your breath.

But breathing is a natural talent, a lifelong gift whether we appreciate it or not. When we become more consciously aware of our breath, we can use it to our advantage. It's a vital source of information. "When I realized I was breathing so shallowly, I knew how much stress I was under." "I was almost out of breath, rushing to fit one more appointment into my day." "I guess I had been holding my breath, waiting to get the test results." You may enjoy a new sense of control over your body as you experiment with regulating this remarkable resource, your personal flow of air.

## Restoratives for the Mind

Contemplation may sound ethereal, but it really grounds you in the here and now. It's almost a restorative for the mind—the mind that has been so busy, perhaps so driven, for so long. "Mind," you might say, "just hang out. Don't go anywhere in particular, just drift." If you prefer to mull something specific, that's fine, too, but make sure no PowerPoint slide or must-do ticklist emerges out of the silence.

There is one caution to observe. If your attempt at contemplation takes you into the past and you find yourself recycling your regrets and your errors—that's not contemplation; it's obsessing. And obsessing serves absolutely no purpose; the only recourse is to cease and desist. You may be someone who does best with contemplation of something outside yourself: dew on the leaf of a plant, a Bach concerto, or replays in your mind's eye of your favorite team's recent win. For some people, movement makes it easier. You can walk or ride or swim while contemplating. Just don't drift too far into the next lane.

When you were younger, you may have explored the world eagerly, ranging far and wide around the globe. Or, possibly, your idea of a big trip was the two-hour drive to your cousin's house. Whatever your roaming style, advancing age may inhibit that previously enjoyed ease of travel. You can blame your body's quirks, your available energy, your bank account—or all of the above. Contemplation offers you another version of travel, revisiting adventures of your past with no ticket required. In this variation, you call up memories from your stash of images. That first time you left home, took a train, flew in a plane. The scenery you saw, the people you met along the way. Remember something you did for the first—perhaps the only—time in your life. Remember something you ate. Remember your effort to communicate in another language, and smile at your attempt.

Since childhood, Sonja had spent nearly all of her vacations at a family cottage on a northern lake. At age 74, her mobility was compromised, to the extent that getting there was increasingly difficult. Friends knew it was a loss for her and sympathized. But she assured them, "I go there every day." She did indeed, in her mind. She had mastered the art of reminiscence.

You're contemplative when you don't rush to judgment on some pressing matter but let it rest unsolved in your mind for some moments—maybe a whole afternoon—before taking action. You're contemplative when you come upon an image or scene that pleases you and you let it become a screensaver for your mind. You're contemplative when you let a piece of chocolate melt in your mouth for several minutes, savoring the taste before you reach for another. You're contemplative when you take time washing your hands and notice how the soap bubbles. You're contemplative when you slow down, soften your gaze, hum a tune.

Meditation is another form of reflection, akin to contemplation but more purposeful, less free-form. Some people meditate to clear the mind of its detritus, seeking to achieve a state of relaxation and calm. Some people meditate in pursuit of a spiritual goal, be it contact with a higher power or worship of a divine presence. While you need only to give yourself permission to indulge in contemplation, meditation requires some discipline or diligence. It's a practice requiring practice. While some long-time meditators can travel beyond the conscious mind with no guideposts for the journey, most people need a bit more structure, some kind of format.

There's sitting meditation, in which you make yourself comfortable in a chair or on a cushion, close your eyes, and devote your attention to your breath. Inhale and exhale consciously, slowing down from the rhythm of daily life. You may accompany the breath with words that appeal to you, one for the in-breath and one for the out-breath. Or choose a mantra, which just means a short phrase that you repeat over and over. Some experimentation is essential. It can take a few tries, rejecting the mantras that serve only to further stimulate your thoughts until you settle on one that is soothing. The time frame for your meditation is also a work in progress. You might set a timer so you don't have to pay attention to the clock. You could aim to sit for three minutes at the start and extend the time as you develop this skill. Because, as I said, it's a practice requiring practice. (We'll visit this topic again in Chapter 14.)

In walking meditation, a slow and gentle pace helps to calm the mind. It's important to choose a destination in advance, along a route that is easy to follow and—as much as possible—free of obstacles. This is a walk, not a hike, and it's a walk that's an end in itself rather than a means to arrive somewhere. In sitting meditation, you maintain a steady awareness of your breath. In walking meditation, you pay close attention to your locomotion, step by step. And in place of repeating words or a phrase, observe your

104   DO LESS. BE MORE.

surroundings. You are the lens of a camera, recording what you see as you pass by.

If you're not so mobile, there's a variation on walking meditation worth trying. Visualize yourself on a moving runway—the sort you find in big airports, only better. Let that runway glide gently and smoothly under you, in your imagination, and pretend that you are walking. Breathe consciously as you "walk," slowing down as you approach the end of your "runway."

There's another kind of meditation that requires no physical effort. Listening meditation is just what the name implies. Make yourself comfortable and set that timer for a few minutes. Close your eyes. Then tune in to all the sounds around you, whatever they may be. It can seem counterintuitive if you've always believed that meditation meant ignoring all distractions. Now you welcome the thrum of the air conditioner, the babble on the street, the thwock of your dog's tail. The buzz of your smartphone, even though you've set it on Silent. (Don't pick up.) Simply listen and savor the respite from your thoughts.

## The Present Moment

What does meditation offer as you age? At the very least, it's a way to live in the present moment, offering a time-out from daily cares and woes. It can provide diversion and even some relief for those suffering from persistent physical discomfort or pain. And for those who seek it, meditation is a pathway to a spiritual realm.

How do you learn to meditate? Time was when you had to sign up for a course, read a book, or seek a guru. Now technology eases the process with apps that guide and encourage you. You can tune in to a soothing voice and, over time, learn to tune out any interruptions that break the spell. You may be surprised by how well you can calm your mind and rest your body in only a few minutes a day. It's not the holy grail of enlightenment that you're after—just some tranquil moments in time.

Those moments matter. As his 90th birthday approached, Dwight said sadly, "I have no future, only my past." He was right, in an actuarial way, that his future is limited. He was correct in owning his past, a past that is rich with ambitions realized—albeit with some dreams deferred. But he missed an important point. He has the here and now, the present moment.

When your focus is the here and now, whether you contemplate or meditate you are practicing mindfulness—an attitude of acceptance of the thoughts, feelings, or bodily sensations that arise when you are in a reflective mode or mood. Mindfulness is attractive to the middle-aged as well as millennials, but old age brings an amplitude of time and experience that can inform your exploration of these states of non-doing and give them depth. Maybe you're seeking stillness, living and breathing gently in the present moment. Maybe your quest is to discover some truth about the cosmos and your place in it. Maybe you just need to relax.

When we were younger, Nike exhorted us to "Just Do It." And we did, over and over, striving and sometimes making our marks. But as you grow older, the balance may shift. Take time to experiment and see how it feels, when you give yourself permission to do less. And be more.

## The New Normal

Along with these expeditions to places where your mind hasn't dwelled before—or stayed very long—you may experience a shift in your attitude about aging. Whatever resistance you have mounted in the past, however reluctant you have been to embrace this stage of life, you become more accepting. Instead of reacting to each unwanted development with alarm (the body letting you down, the mind slipping a bit), you arrive at a new sense of what's normal.

This doesn't happen overnight. The best option is to remain open to the possibility, to the evolution of your self-image. People will continue to ask the usual questions: "What are you up to these days?" "What are you doing?" Maybe your response is thoughtful and authentic: "I'm adjusting. I'm trying to simply be the person I've become, the person I am now."

But to make it more intriguing, that new-normal-for-me person is in some ways just the same as he or she has always been. Maybe you've heard descriptions of this sort: "Really, I feel like I'm my seven-year-old self, except for the aches and pains." "I still care about some of the things I was so fond of when I was four—and I still hate green vegetables." "My family thinks I've become more tolerant, more patient, the older I get. But I think that's the real me. There's just so much that got in the way."

We may not grow taller as we grow older—in fact, we may lose a little height—but we continue to evolve in many other ways. Old age is not that boring plateau I imagined when I was younger. It can be more interesting when you maintain your self-awareness, the recognition of that person you have always been and the person you are now. It can be more rewarding when you take the opportunity to put everything else aside, breathe gently, and dwell in the present moment.

# 13

# WARRANTY EXPIRING

What's happening with that body of yours as you grow older? You can be healthy, maybe even wealthy, and certainly wise—but some changes are taking place without your permission. And even if you work hard to outwit them.

At first, it's gradual. Maybe it's about energy, a realization that you played with your usual enthusiasm but were not at the top of your game. Maybe it's about locomotion—your right knee has developed a mind of its own and just won't function properly. Maybe it's about flexibility—trying to touch your toes takes a little more effort than before, and you may not get very far. Maybe it's about coordination—you were so agile, such a physical multitasker, and you are losing that edge.

Some of the unwanted developments can be identified quite specifically. Others are in that vague category of aches and twinges, minor glitches, and the hard-to-describe. The operating system just isn't what it used to be and there's no update to install.

Of course, some of these setbacks can be diagnosed and treated by medical professionals. Once you reluctantly conclude that a problem isn't going away, you probably visit at least one of those practitioners. In the quest to figure out what's gone rogue in your body, you may even seek opinions from specialists. As we grow older, our list of contacts expands to include consultants with expertise in particular areas—including some we've never heard of before—whether we opt for traditional or alternative medicine.

For many, there's a learning curve to interacting comfortably with providers of medical care. Some people—perhaps more women than men—have developed familiarity with doctors over the years. They have experience with initiating and maintaining those relationships, a sometimes tricky balance between staying open and trusting while asserting their own needs. Other older people are wary of encounters with medical professionals. Maybe it's related to a childhood injury or illness, or issues with authority figures, or simply feeling vulnerable.

It's almost inevitable that your involvement with the world of health care will increase as you age. Some of the engagement will be intimate and personal, related to the rapport between you and your medical advisors, the extent to which you feel understood and respected. Other hoops-to-jump-through pertain to the complex ways that health care services are delivered, a confusing web of preexisting conditions, portals, and pharmacy plans. What sort of practice or clinic or health organization will you select? What are your choices in regard to insurance, the coverages and benefits? Bottom line, how will you pay the bills?

Navigating the health care system isn't fun. As with any endeavor, preparation helps. This may include internet research on what's ailing or troubling you—though it's best to think of such research as background information rather than definitive. The same is true of your conversations with concerned family members or friends. Most important, be sure to write down your questions and concerns in advance of any medical appointments and refer to those notes when you're talking with your physician or other professional. Good advice, at any age.

If you're anxious—and your short-term memory isn't at its best these days—take someone with you to your doctor visits. Maybe you're fortunate enough to have a close friend or family member available. Or you draft someone you don't know quite as well, that nice neighbor who knew you were dealing with some kind of health problem and said, "Oh, I wish I could do something for you." There is. This person can serve as your ally and secretary, taking notes (or recording, with permission) the important points of the consultation. You may be uncomfortable asking this kind of favor. That's understandable, but keep in mind that it is an honor to be invited into someone's rather private world, and to feel trusted. We all need to be needed.

If these appointments and recommendations and treatments bring relief, we're grateful. If not—if the problems are mainly related to our stage of life—we need to design interventions of our own. As my friend Edna, a woman in her mid-80s, says, "You adapt." And when that's not sufficient? "Adapt some more."

What does adaptation mean? It begins with acknowledging that you've sought help and the problem or issue persists. The next step is harder to take: arriving at the realization—the acceptance—that whatever is troubling or bothering or limiting you is a consequence of age. We would rather believe that our back feels funny because we need a new mattress or that sex didn't go as well as usual because we enjoyed a little too much wine the night before. In other words, a one-off—or at least something we can try to attribute to circumstances other than the aging of our bodies.

After acceptance comes a different challenge. You have a choice to make. You can remain discouraged and frustrated about the change in your physical capacity, the disruption in the reliable ways your body has always functioned. Or you can be willing to modify your expectations. You can be ingenious in developing workarounds, those experiments with different ways to cope with your limitations. Some workarounds are in the realm of common sense. Others make use of technology, from apps and other software to the hardware known as assistive devices. Adapt, and adapt some more.

## Working with Workarounds

What's the simplest example of a workaround? The nap. When energy declines, when you can no longer count on a late-afternoon surge of productivity, when familiar night-time sleep patterns are altered ... you can take a nap. A power nap for ten minutes, or a proper nap that's somewhat longer but not so long that you're disoriented when you wake up. Refreshing your system is the goal, enhancing your ability to press on with the rest of the day and evening.

Some workarounds require strategic planning. You can tackle the most demanding tasks of the day at the time you feel most energetic. In keeping with the reality that your need for services is gradually overtaking your wish to acquire more worldly goods, you can think about outsourcing a chore or two. If your hearing isn't what it used to be, you can opt for the quieter restaurant when friends ask where to meet. If your memory is unreliable these days, you can write things down, from to-do lists to weekly calendars to the name of that movie you heard about yesterday but won't recall tomorrow. You can choose paper and pencil or a note-taking app or a voice memo to yourself, whatever works best. Sometimes you need them all.

And some workarounds require accessories. That would include eyeglasses, of course, which you may have worn forever. But if you're having trouble reading fine print or you can't see the street sign (or you came much too close to that dressed-all-in-black cyclist in the dark intersection), maybe you need a new prescription. Even if you've gone through life with 20/20 vision, it's time to reassess. Consider a larger typeface on whatever device you prefer for reading, or order your library book in the large-print version or the audio. Easy workarounds, and not unduly expensive.

For many women and men, eyeglasses have been essential equipment since middle age, even earlier. Not so with hearing aids, which carry a stigma that's hard to overcome. Hearing loss is probably the element of oldness that is most often denied by the owner of the ears. Somehow it seems preferable to repeat "What?" over and over again in a conversation—or miss out on valuable information—than to succumb to that little piece of hardware that amplifies sound. Really, it's just another form of adaptation, an auditory workaround. Think about all those young people sporting gadgets in their ears. Think about the fact that you can regulate the volume and manage other features of today's hearing aids with your phone, which may already have status as your number-one assistive device. Hearing aids aren't perfect and the best ones aren't cheap, but they are worth a trial.

On the topic of stigma, consider aids to mobility, the workarounds that allow you to get around. Hiking poles, canes, and walkers serve a vital purpose if your locomotion is compromised. They allow you to adapt to your body's reality, to do things and go places you might otherwise avoid. It may be hard to let go of your concern about how others see you, but you need to decide just how much a random stranger's perception of you as an old person really matters.

Even if you're better at watching sports than playing them, some kind of physical exercise is vital to maintaining good health as you age. Maybe you fit the description of that line attributed to Mark Twain (among others): "Whenever I feel the urge to exercise, I lie down until it passes." Over the years, you've heard the voices of authorities encouraging—or pressuring—you to get up and get moving. But this may be your last call to start treating your body as something other than a stand for your head. When you explore the many possibilities for shaping up or working out, mobilize your self-awareness. It's the same process you follow with any decision when you are older and wiser: choose something consistent with what you already know about your strengths, your foibles, your lifestyle. Then think in terms of some activity as always better than none. It could even become the practice you've been meaning to adopt.

On the other hand, if you have been an athlete or even a wannabe, adaptation may mean rethinking your goals, the ones that have kept you aiming for your personal bests over a lifetime. Whether you don't run as hard or as long, opt for lighter weights or skip some yoga poses, you can still stay in the game.

This notion of staying in the game applies surprisingly well to sexual activity. The cycle of desire, pleasure, and satisfaction changes with age. Hormones don't fire up the libido as reliably as they once did, back in the day. Bodies don't look the same or respond as easily. The pace is different. There may be more longing for intimate touch, less emphasis on reaching orgasm.

Many women and men are highly motivated to keep their sexuality alive and well at any age. They are happy to revise some of their expectations and willing to experiment with various workarounds. They need no permission to remain sexually active, only a positive attitude about adaptation. Others decide that sex has lost not only some of its intensity, but also some of its significance. Perhaps they grieve the loss of that dimension of their lives. At best, they find some poignant pleasure in remembering their sexual past, calling up images from their personal erotica. A private workaround? Why not?

When we were young, we took our bodies for granted. They did what we wanted them to do, with little conscious thought or effort. As we grow older, we become more aware of the gaps between our hopes and wishes and our capabilities. Coming to terms with this reality inspires our efforts to adapt. We negotiate with ourselves, though it may not be easy. Maybe we give up jogging and switch to power walking. Maybe we mourn for our lost inner athlete and settle for nine holes of golf with a cart. Maybe we revise some scenes in our sexual playbook. But if we are willing to make adjustments, we are likely to find that the assets still exceed the liabilities on our physical balance sheet.

## Coping

Years ago, when I was only in my 40s, I lost the tip of a finger in an accident. I was fortunate to get medical help right away. I have full use of my finger. But I can remember how it felt to lose that little part of my body. It was a shock. I tried to talk myself out of having any sort of grief reaction—good heavens, it could have been so much worse, this was not a tragedy, and so on. But the fact was, it was a trauma to give up even a quarter-inch of myself. At the time, I couldn't imagine the consequences of a life-altering diagnosis or a grave injury.

But as the years roll on, that kind of innocence gives way to the realities of the aging process in one way or another. Maybe our bodies have lost resilience; we tire more quickly and heal more slowly. We can no longer confidently assert that we'll get back to normal functioning just as soon as possible after falling on the ice or enduring the course of chemo. To make it worse, it's often not "one damn thing after another"—it's two. Or more. Lying awake in the dark of night, we have doubts about our survival. There's a sense that our warranty has expired.

How do we cope, day in and day out? How do we manage the deep fears that are likely to accompany the malfunctions in our bodies? What if our mobility is severely compromised and we can't freely move about the world? What if moderate discomfort becomes outright pain? What if a condition is chronic, an illness potentially terminal? In such circumstances we are faced with grieving the way things were and will never be again.

Intellectually, most of us have some understanding that ailments of various kinds come with the territory of old age. A certain amount of physical disturbance or cognitive diminishment is unwanted but expected. If we're fortunate, we have gradually relinquished our defenses—maybe we've developed some reliable workarounds and created a "new normal" way of living. But a serious illness or injury can disrupt that adaptive strategy, sometimes dramatically, marking a change in our health status from well to not-well. We may not have the luxury of overcoming denial over an extended period of time. Diagnoses are made and treatments pursued.

Facing the new reality, many people choose to fight it. Consciously or otherwise, they treat the body as their adversary and prepare to wage war. Think how often you've heard a reference to someone "battling" cancer or "struggling with" a critical illness. There's a healthy aspect to this, if you think of a determined will-to-live mobilizing against the forces of decline and deterioration. A hopeful aspect, if you think of the combatant as energized to ward off depression and despair. An understandable aspect, if the motivation is around achieving particular goals—visiting Italy or seeing a grandchild graduate from high school.

When the poet Dylan Thomas urges his father to "rage, rage against the dying of the light," he is referring to death rather than illness or impairment. But the thought is apt, a kind of mantra for those with warrior instincts.

## Another Path

It's quite a different attitude to forgive your body. To let go of your anger and the perhaps unspoken notion that illness or injury is some sort of betrayal. You may start in the same place—a mixture of disbelief and denial that something has gone wrong in the body you inhabit—but you don't feel insulted by it. You're on the same team as your faltering physical self. You might even try to contemplate mind and body as two expressions of the same being.

And when you think about it, how would it be to arrive at the end of your life with the robust health of the average eight-year-old? Somewhere along the line, there have to be some variations, some deviations from that norm. Further along, diminishment. Still further, infirmity of one kind or another is inevitable.

So you accept the likelihood of illness or disability in some form. You don't take it as a reproach or an invitation to skirmish with the forces of evil. Of course, this is easier if the condition is relatively benign, posing no significant threat to the quality or length of your life. When suffering is more profound, we may be able to learn from the fortunate few who make peace with their condition. They describe disease as a great teacher, as distilling what matters and what doesn't. They speak of passing through hell-on-earth to arrive at a new way of experiencing the world, endowed with clarity and resonant with deep emotion.

One thing is true. Even as you can't control what's happening to your body, you can choose the attitude you take toward its decline. You can work at adopting a mindset that gets you through each day, and only that day, one day at a time. You can grieve the loss of various abilities while you embrace the capacities you still possess.

Bill T. Jones, the legendary choreographer, interviewed people who were coping with life-threatening illness. Grounded in his exploration and inspired by his contemplation of their survival, he created a profoundly moving dance-theater piece and called it *Still/Here*. You are, too.

# 14

## STORMY WEATHER

Many of us have an emotional tendency, however slight or pronounced, to feel out of sorts in some fashion. The default position for some people is sadness—a gloomy outlook or a melancholy mood. The sun may be shining but the world seems dark. For others, the prevailing tone is anxious. We fret, we worry, we anticipate worst-case scenarios. Some of us are familiar with both of these emotional states. We experience a shifting mix of moods, baffling ourselves as well as those around us. I'm sure I don't need to tell you that emotional distress comes in many variations over the life cycle; you've lived it.

Ironically, old age presents a distinctive opportunity to manage your moods and achieve a little more emotional equilibrium. It's related to your growing recognition of your mortality. That

## STORMY WEATHER

unappealing word simply indicates that you don't have all the time in the world. That being the case, you might want to claim every present moment, even savoring a few.

### The Here and the Now

It's perfectly true that the future is foreshortened in the sense that it's not forever. But don't forget that you have the here and now.

Living in the here and now sounds simple, but it's actually demanding. It requires us to put all of our focus on the time at hand and to make good use of that time. Some attitude adjustment may be required as well, to clear away the kind of emotional debris that interferes with taking pleasure in the moment. For example, could you forfeit your critical attitude in favor of adaptation? Could you imagine your frustrations giving way to acceptance? And what about letting go of old resentments rather than clutching them so tightly?

Living in the here and now means altering your perspective from the big picture to the small, the global to the village, the forest to the single leaf. Of course you haven't lost your appreciation of things on a larger scale, but you've gained an awareness of the parts that make up the whole. Living in the here and now also means paying attention to your pace. True, the very recognition of mortality prompts some older people to go into high gear, determined to check off items on their bucket list. That's fine. But consider the alternative—that slowing down allows for deepening your experience of each moment that is still available to you. There's a good reason that we associate old age with rocking chairs. If that's too sedentary for you, take walks. If walking is difficult, study the clouds, feel the breeze, pet a dog.

Living in the present moment is not passive. It calls on all your faculties and all your senses. You were good at it, once upon a time, when you were a very small child. It's time to come full circle and embrace it again. That's a privilege of old age.

## Darkness at Noon

But what if a discouraged mood crosses an invisible line, from the transitory and only moderately troubling to a more serious condition? It actively interferes with your daily life. You find no relief. The present moment has little appeal.

You can be depressed over getting old. You can be depressed about your poor health and a feeling that you've lived too long. You can be depressed because you have suffered from depression for years and there's no obvious reason to recover now. Some people maintain that the prevalence of depression declines over the life cycle as aging adults are relieved of some of the obligations of work and family. Others counter that the losses inherent in the later years—the death of family members and close friends, deteriorating physical health or cognitive functioning, threats to financial security—can easily trigger or deepen depressive episodes.

All of these scenarios have some truth to them. How they apply to you depends on who you are. And so does the treatment of depression. Some believe in medication, some favor counseling in various forms, and some endorse a combination of the two.

While researchers and practitioners continue to search for definitive solutions to depression—which may not arrive in your lifetime, if ever—you can engage in your own effort to lighten your mood. It's not a cure-all or a substitute for traditional approaches. In fact, this strategy is quite compatible with taking prescription medications, exploring your childhood fears, or reframing your negative thoughts.

First, your attitude. You don't have to cheer up. More importantly, don't let anyone else try to cheer you up. This may be counterintuitive, but it matters. Whether you put the burden on yourself to grin while bearing it, or well-meaning friends and family members try to jolly you into a good mood, that doesn't help. Because the disconnect between the way you are feeling—depressed—and the ideal way to feel—not depressed—is simply too great. You can't reach that goal except in very small steps, and it makes you feel worse to gaze up at the mountain.

It also makes you feel alone, even alienated, when people fail to respect the emotional state you are in. Depression is a lonely affair to begin with. Of course people who love you want to instill hope for better days ahead. And that's fine, as long as the expression of hope is preceded by acceptance of the way things are for you, right now.

Which brings us to strategic planning, the antidepressant version in which you learn to plan your life. Each day of it, hour by hour.

Planning is deliberate—the structuring of your life into very small segments or increments. Planning is effortful; it takes motivation. Planning is ongoing; it requires persistence. Not so easy. But it's free and there are no side effects.

This approach—scheduling your daily activities—is helpful in alleviating depression at any age. It becomes especially valuable in the later years when, typically, the responsibilities of a job and family life are diminishing. Time is no longer at such a premium, which can be liberating. Too much time, on the other hand, can be dispiriting, even demoralizing. But you can manage it.

Write down everything you intend to do in a day and evening, on any scheduler app or piece of paper you choose. This will feel familiar, up to a point, from your hardest-charging days when you kept your appointment calendar up-to-date or risked chaos. The difference now is that you enter into this template even the most minor activities of daily living, such as:

- Brush teeth
- Feed cat
- Make to-do list
- Look for lost earring
- Organize credit card receipts
- Leaf through magazine

- Clean top bureau drawer
- Walk around block
- Fix dinner
- Get ready for bed.

You get the idea.

If you are so discouraged that these activities seem overwhelming, break them down into smaller pieces. If you think you can't get out of bed in the morning, stop thinking of it as one event. Think of it as a series of small successes: stretch, yawn, turn to one side, put one foot on the floor, put the other foot on the floor. Take it slowly, go back to square one if necessary, then try again. When you succeed at sitting upright on the bed, congratulate yourself.

There is a natural fit here with the tendency to recalibrate the meaning and importance of various activities as you grow older. Once upon a time, these mundane or trivial actions or events were viewed as exactly that, hardly worth noting. The older you get, the more you may come to accord them some respect as genuine accomplishments, essential to a life well lived.

Keep in mind that depression is a disorder of mood, not a definition of personality. You feel bad but you are not a bad person. Here's where advancing age exacerbates the problem. For some, it's hard to resist recycling all of the regrets accumulated over the years. For others, the risk is obsessing over dreams that haven't come true. But whether your focus is on genuine errors made or fantasies unfulfilled, these thoughts are useless. Of no value. They make you more depressed. Don't go there. Plan your day.

## Soothe Yourself

You may be all too familiar with one or more of the many forms that anxiety takes. You've experienced it over your lifetime in the form of worry, irrational fears, or obsessional thinking. Or you've

STORMY WEATHER

made it this far, generally calm and resilient, only to be surprised by feelings of uncertainty and vulnerability as you grow older.

Whatever your history, living well in your later years involves learning to soothe yourself. If you were younger, I could make the case for exploring and deconstructing and debunking the thoughts that give rise to your anxious moments or underlie your anxious state. And we could take into consideration other influences or contributions—from parental models to traumatic experiences. These approaches might be helpful, given enough time. But time is in limited supply and you deserve to find relief and, eventually, relaxation.

Relief resides within you, in your breath.

Of course you've always known how to breathe. But have you ever consciously managed your breath? Because taking control of your breath is an excellent way to diminish the out-of-control feeling we call anxiety. You may have experimented with this after reading about "doing" less and "being" more, in Chapter 12. But let's build on it.

Find a comfortable place to sit quietly. Put both feet on the floor, rest your hands on your knees (palms up or down), and close your eyes. Breathe in through your nose and count slowly and silently ... one, two, three. Breathe out through your nose and count slowly and silently ... three, two, one. Repeat. Repeat again. And again.

As you might guess, your goal over time is to deepen the breath to a longer count—adding to your sequence, maybe reaching five or six. Also, as you continue to practice, you can make the exhale a bit longer than the inhale. If your nasal passage is at all constricted, you can breathe out through your mouth.

If you become bored with simple counting, try some variations. Choose words that resonate with you and say them silently with the inbreath and the outbreath: peace/calm, restore/relax. Or imagine that your breath has a beautiful color and infuse your whole body with that color as you breathe deeply in and out.

With practice, see if you can work toward sustaining the experience for three minutes. Initially, set a timer so none of your energy is directed to the clock. Eventually you may not need the timer.

This careful and rhythmic breathing works on anxiety in two ways. Physiologically, you are calming the nervous system, the apparatus in your body that mobilizes in response to perceived threats, real or imagined. Your nerves have put you on high alert. Conscious breathing is one way to ease the tension. Cognitively, you are defeating the negative thoughts that fuel anxiety. You are focusing exclusively on saying the chosen numbers or words to yourself, even as you maintain a vague awareness of the sound and sensation of your breath. Inevitably, you'll shift back into useless obsessing or just ordinary grocery-list-type thoughts. Consider saying to them, aloud if necessary, "Sorry, you'll have to wait." Go back to your breath.

The key is practice. Keep in mind that you can do this almost anywhere, at any time.

Conscious breathing is especially helpful with anticipatory anxiety—the fear or dread of something yet to come—and to some extent with defeating recurrent and troubling thoughts from the past. It gives you a safe place to retreat and restore yourself.

Many older people find themselves preoccupied with their past mistakes, real or imagined, and suffer from the kind of guilt that keeps on giving. If there's something to undo or apologize for, by all means make amends. More often your mind gets stuck in a continuous loop that replays these errors of omission and commission to no purpose, except for making you miserable. There's a way to interrupt those thoughts, at least temporarily.

Go back to your comfortable sitting position. Close your eyes and imagine that you are standing in an elevator on the top floor of a tall building. You are alone, except for your baggage—your troubled thoughts. Picture yourself pressing the button and descending one level. The doors open. Now you stay in the elevator but toss out one of the things you most regret—something painful that has bothered you for a very long time—onto the floor. You leave it there, the doors close, you descend again. Floor by floor, you throw your unwanted emotional baggage out of the elevator.

Stay with this image until you feel a little relief or a slight sense of accomplishment. Either one is better than lugging those bags around.

Finally, you might want an alternative for those times when you don't have the patience to slow down and enjoy something as deliberate and restful as breathing or as creative as imagery. It's even simpler, really. You can counter your anxiety through deliberate action.

Do something. Do anything. It helps if it's physical to some extent, but that can mean sitting up instead of lying down, walking twice around a room instead of standing still. When you feel jittery or fearful, it's tempting to believe that you are beset by feelings beyond your control. It's not true. You can alter your experience of the moment, in the moment, by taking some kind of action, however inconsequential it may seem. Pour yourself a glass of water. Stretch your arms over your head as far as they will go. Look out the window. Do something.

Whether your distraction takes the form of breathing, imagery or a simple action, the respite won't last indefinitely. That's life. But you'll have some tools to help you cope.

# 15

## YOU AND YOUR CONSTANT COMPANION

Drinking to excess … smoking … overeating … internet porn and other obsessions … perhaps you're all too familiar with behavior that's hard to control. If not, you get a pass from reading this short chapter.

But if you are habituated, or addicted, or in some way dependent on a substance or an activity that you know is not in your best interest, this is for you.

Here's the thing about compulsive behavior as you grow older: you and your behavior have probably been together for a long time. You're old friends. That's a big part of the problem. In a time of life that's marked by losses of all kinds, imagine giving up something

126 YOU AND YOUR CONSTANT COMPANION

you've grown so close to, relied upon. Something so familiar, so readily available. Why would you want to do that?

That's a good question, and it can be a tough one to answer. Let's start by thinking about the consequences of your habit. Does indulgence in the behavior make you feel bad about yourself? Does reliance on it make you feel even worse? Consider, and take note.

Of course your behavior may upset other people, people you care about. If so, I'm sorry, and you may be, too. But the wishes and hopes of others are insufficient motivation for you to abandon the old friend we're talking about. Listen to family members and friends when they express their concern, by all means. But that's not enough, not by a long shot.

No, it's all about you and your self-respect.

What difference does it make, that you're growing older? For one thing, as we've noted, it means you've probably been relying on whatever it is for many years. You're a chronic user, eater ... you name it. And over time you may have tried all kinds of strategies to kick the habit. Repeatedly.

Not such a good prognosis, is it?

But there's one big difference as you approach old age. Time is limited. This is likely to be your last chance to feel differently about yourself. I'm not talking about improving your health or your marriage. If those objectives were compelling you would have kicked the habit long ago. I'm talking about putting an end to the disrespect and the self-loathing, the depression and the despair.

If that has any appeal, you might want to think about ending the relationship with your companion while you still have some time left. It's beyond the scope of this book to lay out a complete program for treating compulsive behavior of any kind, but I can help you make a start.

Timing. Life at this point is not a dress rehearsal. The future is not stretching out before you to a limitless horizon. It's finite. As the cliché has it, if not now, when? Let's explore this. If you're honest, what's your image of a life well lived and how does that square with the life you're leading now? Is that good enough for you? When did you imagine you might do something about the discrepancy?

That's looking ahead. What if you look back? Do you think you haven't smoked enough cigarettes? Drunk enough booze? Watched enough X-rated videos? Of course you can continue. But let's wonder if the experience will be significant, let alone profound or even distinctive. By definition, old habits aren't very interesting. Some are quite boring.

By contrast, consider the adventure of ending any relationship. Yes, it's scary and lonely, but you may feel very much alive, vulnerable to all kinds of emotional twists and turns. It's the same with letting go of a cherished compulsion. However self-defeating the activity may be, you've valued its availability, its dependability in your times of need—just like any other flawed but secure attachment in life.

About the scary part: you'll need ways to fill the time, find substitutes for whatever it was you were doing (and doing and doing). You'll be giving up a pattern of behavior that was entirely familiar and reliable. You'll be confronting a void and you'll be anxious. So you'll have to learn to predict the pitfalls and to plan—carefully and purposefully—in order to successfully maneuver around them.

As for the lonely part, a solution is obvious. Don't try to do this by yourself. If you've managed to keep the behavior a secret (at least you think it's a secret), you'll have to come clean with at least one person, preferably more. It's likely that your troubled and troubling behavior is known to others. Some of them may be ready to help. Others may be as averse to change as you have been, and possibly threatened by your determination to defeat the demon. Choose wisely. You need allies, a support system. Think about connecting with a 12-step program or any other group that promotes recovery.

As you probably know by now, whether you are dealing with an entrenched habit or a long-standing addiction, a change of this

## YOU AND YOUR CONSTANT COMPANION

kind is profoundly challenging. It's an effort that requires mobilizing your energy and your determination, your patience and your resolve.

So you need to be realistic, to consider whether this challenge is right for you. It may not be. But contrary to popular wisdom, old age offers opportunities to make choices, to take control of some aspects of your life. It just doesn't keep the window open indefinitely.

At the very least, this pattern of behavior that has power over you has become rather automatic. Do yourself the favor of becoming explicit about it. Bring it into sharp focus, claim it as yours—and make a deliberate decision about its place in your old age.

As a first step in the process, listen to a few people struggling with the issue of dependency as they grew older. Maybe you'll identify, maybe one of their stories could be yours.

Harry reflects on a turning point in his drinking life:

*When I woke up the morning after my sixtieth birthday celebration, I had a terrible hangover. The day was pretty much lost, except for one thing. I got to thinking about my father, who died last year. He was what they used to call a functional alcoholic. He never lost a job, didn't beat his wife. But his life was largely organized around having his drinks. That seemed to be what mattered most, even more than spending time with us kids.*

*I've been drinking the way he did most of the time, but some binges like the night of the party really scared me. I don't know yet if I will have to give it up entirely but I know something has to change.*

Jane describes her relationship with prescription pills:

*I wouldn't have called it an addiction until recently. I needed medication to manage my pain after an awful car accident in my 20s. But that was a long time ago. What I'm doing right now is*

YOU AND YOUR CONSTANT COMPANION   129

*admitting to the way I've been misusing meds. I take pills to calm me down, and I take pills to speed me up. I look so healthy and fit in my 60s, I've even succeeded in talking more than one doctor into writing me another prescription. As you might guess, I have other sources, too. I feel trapped, and I want out. Not sure how to do it but I don't like this image of myself. Especially as I look ahead.*

Stanley started gambling when he was a teenager. Today, almost fifty years later, the stakes are much higher:

*Yes, it's a compulsion but I love the risks. Of course I love the highs, but even the lows set me up to get back in the game again. I've been really lucky, sticking mostly—but honestly, not completely—to legal betting. Maybe I should worry about getting in trouble with the law, but I'm really much more concerned about running out of money before I die. My wife knows about my habit, but not the extent of it. I never gave this much thought when I was younger. Now I'm anxious about the future. This can't go on. I may need some help.*

Harry, Jane, and Stanley are each taking a hard look at their past history and their present situation. They are owning up to their distress over their behavior, admitting that there is a problem. By arriving at this point—no longer fooling themselves about the toll taken by their dependency—they are overcoming their denial.

This first step, this moment of clarity, is essential to making any revision of your life's script. It allows you to wonder if your future might somehow be different, even if the outcome can't be predicted yet. Harry, Jane, and Stanley may follow different paths in the days ahead. What they share is the realization that they have choices to make as they face growing older. If you have a constant companion, think about your own choices. While there's still time.

# 16

## THE SIGNIFICANCE OF OTHERS

As the wise yoga teacher Max Strom has noted, there is no app for happiness. Maybe not, but that doesn't keep people of all ages from searching for it. Particularly when this elusive happiness is represented by a loving connection to another person. Or more than one.

The quest for connection, be it romantic or platonic, sexual or spiritual, is a constant theme in our earlier years. Most of us have a drive, sometimes compelling, to seek a mate or partner; most of us have a powerful yearning to be chosen by someone to whom we are attracted. And with very few exceptions, we need companionship. We don't want to go through life entirely alone. So we overcome our insecurities or inhibitions and work at forming

## 132 THE SIGNIFICANCE OF OTHERS

relationships. Classmates, friends, neighbors. Colleagues. Extended family members. Online contacts. Supermarket checkers.

The degree of closeness varies greatly, of course. Some people do best keeping their connections at arm's length while others crave intimacy. The selection process varies, too. Some tend to connect with others of the same ilk—age or gender, education or interests—while others enjoy the stimulation of differences.

Connecting in later life shares some of these universal qualities. But it also has a special poignancy, created in large measure by the losses we are sustaining. The rate of attrition in our cohort steps up. We lose family members, life partners, best friends. It can take courage to reach out again, to risk being vulnerable, to let others know you.

So unless you are an extrovert blessed with unwavering optimism, making connections can be difficult. It takes initiative. Little wonder that the default position of many older people is to withdraw into their own skin or settle for the secure base of a trusted few. Also consider that our emotional defenses—which may once have served as strong and sturdy bulwarks against rejection or disappointment—are often diminished as we age.

You can't replace the people you have loved dearly and deeply. There are no substitutes. But oldness offers a kind of compensation, if you are willing to be flexible with your expectations. Relationships in the earlier stages of life are apt to be characterized by their intensity. We looked for that vital spark of shared interests and tastes, common values. We were energized by these connections, often felt more alive. If the pairing was romantic, there was a crazy-in-love thrill; if the encounters were sexual, there was passionate excitement, a feeling beyond your control.

Life changes, and so can you. It requires a shift in your emphasis, in revising the considerations you make in the process of reaching out. When you were younger, many of your interpersonal

THE SIGNIFICANCE OF OTHERS    133

connections were based on similarity, some identification with the other person. That felt good. As you age, you can become less particular, more open to differences. Less exclusive, more inclusive of people unlike yourself. The goal is not to replicate your own attributes in someone else, but to enjoy some simple camaraderie, that we're-all-in-this-world-together feeling. These companionable interactions serve to buffer the feelings of loneliness so prevalent in later life.

As one example, take note of the way the age factor in relationships evolves slowly over the life cycle. As children or teenagers, every year matters. Do you remember when you thought the girls two grades ahead of you were a different species? Or as a young adult, the whiff of scandal that went with dating out of your age range, seeing someone much older? As the years go by, these distinctions lose some of their relevance. Think how often you don't remember a person's age—if you ever knew it.

You may want to pay more attention to the outer circle of your social universe. I'm referring to the people who populate your daily life, the people with whom you have brief encounters of all kinds. When you were younger, you may not have made time to connect with the UPS driver or the barista, even as they were essential to your well-being. Now it's satisfying— and hardly effortful—to engage in a little conversation when you receive a package, a little banter when you place your order at the coffee shop. As you age, you'll need more assistance from people in various helping roles. Take time to be interested and appreciative—and make those relationships matter.

## You and Your Friends

What about the meaningful connections that are already in place, the friendships that may be relatively recent or, more likely at this

## 134 THE SIGNIFICANCE OF OTHERS

point, the ones that have a long history? Age has a bearing in a number of ways, some welcome and others somewhat perverse. For example, it's essential to make allowances for encroaching old-ness. Aging friends forget the lunch date or get the time wrong. They can't find a parking place and if they do, they can't remember where the car is when they come out of the restaurant.

Friends tell long stories you have already heard, more than once. People who once engaged you in intense conversation about world events now report their blood pressure readings or how they really should find another physical therapist. All kinds of foibles. You have your own, of course.

But most of this age-related behavior isn't directed at you per-sonally, even if you feel momentarily disappointed or disrespected. Whatever the misunderstanding, however long you stand by the movie theater box office wondering if your friend will show up, it's probably not about you. It's that old devil, age.

It comes as no surprise that the character of friendship alters with the advancing years to include a large element of caretaking. It isn't only the conversation that changes, it's the needs that people—includ-ing you—have as they grow older. Roles change. You may be counted on for emotional support in all kinds of situations. It may be hands-on care for the friend recovering from a knee replacement or transporta-tion for the neighbor undergoing cancer treatment or the meal you prepare and deliver to the newly widowed. The range of events calling out for your empathy and understanding expands and the frequency increases. Rather than responding to an occasional call for help, you're in it for the longer haul. At the same time, you hope for—you deserve—some sympathetic attention to whatever is going on in your own life.

Oldness, when you think about it, is a persistent condition. Factor in illness or injury, either of which can be acute or chronic, sometimes one leading to the other. Friendship has always been

THE SIGNIFICANCE OF OTHERS          135

a mutual arrangement; now there's a more significant element of taking turns, responding to each other's needs as they arise.

It's fine to bring some selectivity to your friendship ties. Some connections are really situational. The two of you became acquainted in some shared circumstance and thought you had a lot in common, but the relationship isn't standing the test of time. There's no dishonor in withdrawing from that involvement, although it may not be easy. Or a long-running friendship has caused you more anxiety than satisfaction over the years and you're simply tired of holding up your end. You don't have to say goodbye. But if you bring your behavior more into sync with your feelings, it probably means a little less contact.

On a more positive note, people often report a deeper recognition of the value of friendship as they get older. The notion that originated in the gay and lesbian community a few decades ago, that friends can constitute a highly desirable family-of-choice, has gone mainstream. We're all the better for it.

For the most part, we're taking stock here of connections to people who are more or less in your age range, and that's fine. It's also essential that you, as an older person, have some younger acquaintances or friends. Forget the nonsense about proximity to youth keeping you young. Envying the six-pack abs of a 30-year-old man or admiring the dewy complexion of a 20-something young woman hardly makes your years fade away. Instead, it's the contrast in our lives—young and old—that's so informative and stimulating. We get to find out what's going on in the world from which we are gradually withdrawing. We get to watch the way young lives unfold, with all the similarities and differences from our own.

What do we give in return? If we're asked, we give wise counsel. But we need no invitation to take young people seriously and offer emotional support. Unlike other authority figures prominent in their

136    THE SIGNIFICANCE OF OTHERS

lives, we don't evaluate, we don't criticize, we don't put any conditions on the relationship. As older people, we're simply there for them. It matters not that we may dislike their music and they may not appreciate ours. As I said before: we're all in this world together.

## Intimate Partners

And the people who matter most, the significant others, lovers, spouses? How does old age affect or alter those relationships? As Pamela, the considerably younger wife of an aging husband, put it with a sigh, "I could write a book..." That book would include all the clichés about old age. Forgetfulness, rising impatience, increasing sensitivity, escalating frustration. Some of these effects are related to the aging of the brain; others are consequences of the sense that we are slowly losing our influence in the world, if not our bearings. Regardless of the cause, we don't like what's happening with our dearest companions. Besides, they serve as mirrors of where we are or where we're headed. We don't like that at all.

The reality is that your partner can't help getting older any more than you can. The behavior that irritates or frustrates you isn't willful or intentional. It is what it is—old guy or old lady stuff. Once you cross that threshold, that moment of truth, you are on your way to acceptance. Acceptance doesn't come overnight, though, and even if it did it might not last much past noon. Acceptance depends on your mood, your partner's mood, and all the myriad complications of life. Acceptance may be transient, it may be fragile, but it's crucial to sustaining a close relationship in old age.

Good communication is essential, too. That's always been true, but now there's the more-so phenomenon—whatever a couple's style of conversing, it's apt to be exacerbated as each partner grows older. Bickerers bicker. Stonewallers stonewall. Not to mention the part played by even a minimal hearing loss ... If sensitive issues

THE SIGNIFICANCE OF OTHERS     137

arise late in life, you and your partner may need a refresher course in *Talking to Each Other* (Appendix III).

We all need to grieve for the loss of the way things were. The way he could be counted upon to tackle any household repair project. The way she could be trusted to pay the bills and never see a finance charge. The way turning to each other in bed could make the day's frustrations disappear. Things have changed. They aren't so certain. It's sad, that we mark advancing age by means of these disappointments, but it's real. And so we grieve.

If your partner's health or well-being is compromised in some significant way—it could be a brief episode or longer term—you take on new roles. This may mean assuming responsibilities you never had before, and never wanted. Think about the everyday tasks and errands your partner can no longer manage as physical capacity declines. Consider the contribution to your shared decision-making that is altered when one mind is no longer so reliable, so sharp. Little wonder that the healthier or more functional partner feels burdened by the need, as 75-year-old Arnold put it, "to think for two people." Some say there's a trade-off in this stage, that people are surprised by their ability to adapt to the challenges. They discover a kind of resilience that they never knew they had, or find satisfaction in taking control of confusing situations, or learn to ask for help. True for some. But even with such enviable coping skills, all intimate partners face the hard truth that this transformation of their relationship is demanding. If they made a promise to stick together for better "or worse," here it is.

Then we develop—or hope to develop—tolerance. Tolerance is acceptance buttressed by patience and a touch of grace. It's what we feel when we are at our best and we love with our whole heart. There's an element of fondness, maybe a little humor. Think of how you want your own old-age quirks and diminishments to be treated by someone who loves you. That's your model. Finally, there's gratitude. Maybe you have a little more time together.

138　THE SIGNIFICANCE OF OTHERS

## Family Dynamics

Family relationships go through their own transformations in old age. For some, these really are the ties that bind. At their best, family members recognize that time together is precious. One insight is nearly universal: the realization that parents are growing older and will not be with us forever. This passage-of-time awareness affects same-generation siblings and cousins, too. They find ways to reunite across distance and time zones. They feel a need to touch base in the present and talk about the past, reviewing or reconstructing it. Memory lapses get filled in, misperceptions get revised, funny stories are recycled in the process. It's the family version of life review.

The family system often endures another kind of shift, this one unwelcome. We can predict—even accept—that the older generation will exhibit the signs and symptoms of aging. We're not counting on those relatives to be at full strength, functioning at 100 percent of their capacity. But we're taken aback at the news of ailments or illness suffered by younger members of the family. In a perfect world, they were supposed to be spared the fears and frustrations of any disabling condition. A middle-aged son is diagnosed with Parkinson's. A granddaughter starts on a new medication to control her seizures. Your younger friend—the one you counted on to send you funny memes—is coping with an episode of clinical depression. Sadly, more losses are added to our expanding collection of life experiences.

When your children have children, it's a major shift in the family dynamics. The appearance of a new generation has a profound impact on the senior members. This development may have been long anticipated, hoped for. More than one newly minted grandmother has declared, "Grandparenting is the only experience in life that is even better than imagined." The opportunity to nurture

## THE SIGNIFICANCE OF OTHERS    139

young children without taking complete responsibility for their well-being is welcomed enthusiastically. The doting may be long-distance, aided by Skype, or it may be hands-on, with grandparents assuming a variety of important roles in helping to raise their grandchildren.

Not everyone feels this way about achieving grandparent status, and it can be hard to admit to some ambivalence. Most obviously, it's confirmation of your oldness. Other consequences are more subtle but significant. As 65-year-old Alice described it, "I hate to say it, but I'm done. I raised three children and it was hard work. I love my grandchildren but it's time to take care of myself." At age 71, Warren spoke of enjoying monthly visits with his two grandsons. But he added wistfully, "I can't get used to the loss of time with their dad. He has a new focus, and that's as it should be, but I feel left out." Note, too, the discrepancy between grandparents' expectations and reality. If they hoped to make use of the parenting wisdom they gained over the years, there's inevitable disappointment when their offspring fail to ask for their advice. Or reject it.

Even as family traditions are maintained, roles inevitably change. Sybil, a grandmother of seven, described what she experienced at the family's holiday celebration. "The next generation has taken over! My eldest daughter did all the planning and the grandchildren helped with the cooking. I felt a bit overwhelmed, pleased but overwhelmed. It's odd to say I feel a bit lost in my family but there it is."

A different kind of family connection is retrospective. Many older people experience a growing desire to know more about their history, their family's origins. This interest is in stark contrast to those youthful days when an elderly aunt droned on about her ancestors and you rolled your eyes. Now, whether it involves contacting little-known distant relatives or exploring the internet to create a family tree, genealogy can become a fascinating project to pursue. As

## 140 THE SIGNIFICANCE OF OTHERS

with many endeavors, there are trade-offs. In the best scenarios, this research into one's own history is grounding, offering a more secure sense of identity and belonging. But along the way, some revelations are provocative. You might discover the existence of a half-sister you didn't know about, or learn that your ethnic origins are not what you've always been told. As you proceed, stay aware that surprises may lie ahead.

All families have their share of misfortune, even tragedy. The later years present a dilemma if a family is burdened by conflict or members are estranged. They can seek reconciliation before it's too late, or despair of the possibility. There's sadness in coming to terms with the realization that time is limited, but it may serve as a catalyst for reaching out, in the hope of healing rifts. If not, there will be losses to mourn.

Whatever the history or the prevailing attitudes of the family you grew up in or the one you have created, the family dimension of your life gains prominence as you grow older. Much of that is emotional resonance. When you ponder your experience with the most important figures in your life, it's understandable and normal to feel a mix of pleasure and regret, satisfaction and sadness. Maybe some of your dreams for those relationships came true, some of your hopes were fulfilled. For others, your emotions fall on a continuum from mild disappointment to heartbreak. From the vantage point of advancing age, reflections on family life are apt to have a bittersweet quality. That's reality.

If you have issues of inheritance to resolve at some point in the future, expect some disturbance in your emotional equilibrium. It takes courage to imagine a world without you, even if you hope to live on in people's hearts and minds. But whether you have a fortune to bequeath to lucky beneficiaries or your legacy consists of an old-fashioned set of china and some treasured family photograph albums, the dynamic is the same. You will need to make some decisions about dispersing your assets and sharing your worldly goods.

You do your survivors a favor when you leave specific instructions for after you're gone. It's common knowledge that these directives are supposed to be documented in your will. It's also a simple fact that not everyone is ready to make one. If you are in that category, try an experiment. Think about a niece of whom you are especially fond. Try taping a label—"for Sarah, eventually"—to the back of a picture frame or the bottom of a pottery dish. See how that feels. If it feels all right, you've taken a first step toward making a will.

Another important aspect of family life is practical, as issues of care and responsibility for an aging family member—could be you—arise. In that perfect world, the younger generation plays its part willingly, siblings cooperate harmoniously, and even the more distant relatives come to your aid. But on the planet that most of us inhabit, there are differences of opinion, frustrations and resentments. It helps to keep in mind that there's nothing new here. When one member of a family needs help, old rivalries and tensions resurface. Call them pre-existing conditions. If you are the focus of all this attention, your job is to stay outside the family energy field. Ask for what you need. Let others determine how best to provide it.

Change affects nearly everything as we grow older, and it's true of our relationships. Some attachments become more tenuous, while others deepen and become more profound. Many of these transitions are beyond your control, but others are yours to influence. You play your part when you treat people with respect. When you attend to friends and family members with kindness and tolerance. When you assure your most significant companions of your loyalty and love. Change is inevitable. If you can adapt to it, you can enjoy a measure of happiness, however you define it. Even without an app.

# 17

## LOVES LOST

When you were younger, your world could be turned upside down when you learned of a friend's serious injury or a family member's grave illness, but there was a good chance that you would eventually recover from the shock and regain your equilibrium. As you grow older, your world changes. Although some people manage to reach their later years relatively unscathed, middle age is typically a time of intermittent loss. Then, as you age, the losses are likely to occur with greater frequency—one after another, and sometimes simultaneously.

For nearly everyone, the most painful losses are those of people close to us. But there's no hierarchy of loss, nor should there be. Loss simply means that something has gone missing that was once present and deeply valued. It could be a person, a place, or a thing. It could be a dog or a cat, a house or a car, a bracelet or a pocket-knife. It could be money in the bank or a professional reputation or your good health. Or it could be a long-held dream or fantasy, when you have to accept that it will never come true.

We're all so different. Some people experience the death of a pet with the same intensity as the loss of a parent. Some people react to the loss of a home or the end of a marriage with a similar depth of feeling. You know who you are; you know what causes you to suffer greatly.

Along with our individual vulnerabilities, certain broad themes influence how we respond to a loss. One is proximity. Some people are baffled when they find themselves responding more emotionally to the death of a neighbor than to the loss of their favorite uncle. The reality may be that they loved their uncle dearly but saw him rarely. The neighbor was close at hand. There were many interactions and exchanges, hardly profound but enjoyable. Death cheats us of the camaraderie. Day by day, we experience its absence, and we feel the loss more than we might expect.

Another theme involves your self-esteem. The more you feel identified with a person, a place, or a thing, the more intensely you will feel its absence. When you think about it, this makes emotional sense. A family member or a special friend respects or admires or enjoys you, perhaps all of these. You derive great satisfaction and pleasure, even a sense of worth, from this connection. When this person dies, it may seem that a part of you dies, too. We suffer this most painfully, of course, in the loss of the loved ones closest to our hearts.

Think of other emotional investments that make us feel good about ourselves. You can be bonded to the pet you raised, to the garden you planted, to the institution where you worked for many years. These connections work both ways. If we lose them—a beloved dog dies or we abandon the garden to relocate closer to an

LOVES LOST 145

adult child or we retire from an organization that sustained us in so many ways—we feel the loss deeply. Psychologically speaking, a part of ourselves has gone missing.

Old age also means losing parts of ourselves in a more functional sense. We're at risk for losing some of our autonomy as our minds slip and our bodies falter. We're forgetful at the very least, confused at the worst. We're not as mobile and flexible as we once were. We don't hear or see as well. We tire more easily than we want to admit.

We're also vulnerable to a different kind of loss in old age, dispiriting in its own way: the erosion of our authority or influence in the world. Younger generations are displacing us in the workplace and the wider culture. Whether we like it or not, it's no longer our turn. We would like to consult with the local planning commission, but our official term has ended. We hope to share our wisdom with the new parents, but the advice columnists say we must first receive an invitation to offer guidance—and it can be a long wait.

## Grieving the Losses

If loss—whatever its character—is inevitable in old age, how do we survive? How do we go on without feeling depleted and losing all resilience? How do we persevere and maintain some hope for our own lives? We must grieve our losses. I don't know any other way.

Remember that grief is the tax we pay on our attachments. If we didn't attach, if we didn't engage or relate or identify so profoundly, there would be no tax to pay. The challenge facing us at any age—but especially as we grow older—is how to make those payments.

We begin by making our grief matter to ourselves. It's not as simple as it sounds. Your work—and mourning is hard work—is to recognize your grief, honor it, endure it. You make your grief matter when you spend time, in your imagination or daydreams, with the person, place, or object of your affection. Give yourself permission to reminisce about your initial attraction, to remember what you shared, to recall the milestones. Acknowledge the regrets. Savor the pleasures.

If you are devastated by the sudden death of someone you loved deeply, your grief is immediate and stark. You enter, helplessly, into a dark and empty space. You may lie awake all night or dream strange dreams or lose your appetite. You may feel bruised in body and in mind. For many people, the deprivation—having to go on in life alone—is central. For others, it's more the change in their personal universe, as though their tectonic plates were shifting. There is no one way to feel, and certainly no correct way to feel about the ending of a relationship. The caregiver who has seen someone through a long and devastating illness may feel distraught—and relieved. The partner whose significant other refused to take responsibility for his health may feel bereft—and angry.

Grieving takes many forms. Tears are potent. People sometimes fear that once they begin crying, they will never be able to stop. Your weeping or sobbing may last for a long time, but you will eventually stop—and you will likely feel some relief, each time you cry. If that's not true for you, consider the experience of Rosemary, who lost her husband in a tragic accident: "I was tiring myself out with crying. I started asking myself, 'If these tears were words, what would they say?' Some of the words were angry and some were so sad."

It may help on some occasions to cry in the presence of another person. The witness to your sorrow doesn't need to say anything in particular or say anything at all. It's his or her presence in your time of trouble that matters, a quiet affirmation of your distress.

More of the work of grieving takes place when you tell the story in detail, over and over if need be. Now your witness becomes a listener, and you speak of what or whom you lost, when and where and how it happened. In the case of a sudden and traumatic loss, telling the story can help to take the horror—"the dark blob that blots out everything else," as one therapist calls it—out of the experience. Slowly, piece by piece, you integrate this terrible turn of events into your life, your changed reality.

There are many ways to grieve. Some people express their feelings by creating art, making music, writing poetry—or taking long hikes. Families search for ways to adapt their routines and rituals to the fact that one of their own is missing, neither denying the absence or allowing it to shatter all of their traditions. An empty chair for Grandpa may be placed at the table on that first holiday after the loss. An older sister's birthday may be celebrated by sharing loving memories instead of a cake.

Many grievers find it rewarding to pay tribute to a person they loved or admired in some tangible form. Such memorials can be extravagant. You've read about the wealthy widow who donated a new wing to a hospital in the name of her husband, an expression of gratitude for the good care he received there. Other offerings are simple and heartfelt. Grieving the death of a mother who was passionate about reading, her daughter Tamara designed a memorial bookplate with her mother's name and dates. She pasted it inside the cover of a dozen books—including some by her mother's favorite author—and donated them to the local library. Looking for a way to honor the memory of an old friend, Frank signed up to "Walk for the Cure," an event to fund research on the disease that claimed his good pal. He was glad to make a small contribution each year in the man's name, but knew it was really the walk with other supporters that helped him to grieve.

## 148  LOVES LOST

Most importantly, label grief for what it is. If we believe that it matters—that grief is an inescapable part of being alive—then we learn to take care of ourselves, to resist any pressure to make it go away or to act normal, whatever that is. We may have to turn toward the direction of the skid, so to speak, before eventually pulling out of the icy patch and getting back on the road.

Sometimes grief arrives unannounced and unbidden, a wave of mourning that overwhelms you when the finality of a loss sinks in, perhaps months or even years later. The prompt may be a holiday, a loved one's birthday, a trip to your old hometown, or a song from the '60s on Pandora. A loss may be revisited and grief revived over a very long period of time. There is no universal timetable.

When the death is that of a loved one, the rituals of a culture or faith may surround and uphold the griever. Some mourning traditions have been abandoned or revised in contemporary society—the black armband is no more—but other customs endure and comfort. What matters is the affirmation of the grieving that is taking place. The sympathy can arrive in the form of a casserole or a green plant. It can come as a fond recollection of the one who passed away, shared in person or posted online.

It's different when the loss you suffer is not known to others. With a lifetime of experiences, some older people have attachments that are private, even secret. When these come to an end, grief can be especially lonely.

The loss of close friends is a common and poignant experience in old age. Maybe these are friendships enjoyed over a lifetime, forged in the halls of high school and strengthened ever since. Or a friendship made more recently in the retirement community dining room, where you were beguiled by your table companion's warmth and wit. Unlike family members, these are the people we have actually chosen to make part of our lives. We have invested emotionally, but selectively. These are our peers, and we felt we were all in this together, until one departs. And, all too often, another. Along with missing our companions, there's the almost-the-same-age factor playing its part here: the heightened awareness that our turn will come, too.

Grieving is really a long, slow process of transforming real people and places, real objects and experiences, into memories. Symbols can help us in this journey. We do well when we can hold on to something that represents our loss. My washing machine broke down some years ago. I couldn't fathom how many loads of family laundry it had washed and rinsed; I only knew a deep well of sadness when it died. Of course, it wasn't the machine itself; it was what it represented—my years of raising a family, with all the trials, tribulations, and joys. Before it was carted away to make room for its replacement, I managed to remove the control panel and I kept it for a long time as a memento. Strange to you, I'm sure, but satisfying for me. Grieving takes many forms.

## What It Means

As for the meaning of your grief, the possibilities are wondrous. Maybe it's about your capacity to love so deeply. Maybe it's about discovering your ability to survive despair. Maybe it's about learning lessons that you can take forward in your own life.

Or, instead, the meaning may be about the object of your love. You may come to a fresh appreciation of the qualities that bound you to her—or him, or it—in the first place. You may even acknowledge the things that weren't so appealing. Eventually, the separation in time and space helps to resolve those seeming disparities. Best of all, you might discover—perhaps to your surprise—that you have appropriated some admirable trait of the one you loved and made it part of yourself.

Or the meaning may be in yet another realm, evolving out of your status as a survivor of life's tragedies. It could come in a moment of philosophical awareness or as a spiritual revelation that sustains you. Whatever form it takes, the meaning emerges from your grief and stays close to your heart.

The taxman will come around again, alas, but you know how to pay.

# 18

## WHEN IT ALL FALLS APART

And it probably will. You don't know when. But in this process of growing older—no matter how careful, how deliberate, how creative you may be at living into your advancing age—things are apt to fall apart at some point in time. For whatever reason, some aspects of your life that once seemed stable or at least predictable will have become precarious.

It could be one unexpected development that puts you over the emotional edge. Or a series of disturbing events for which you were unprepared. Too many, too much.

Most crises involve loss of some kind, some variation from what was known and familiar and moderately secure. Your health, your finances, your relationships, your living situation—possibly all of the above—are in some kind of jeopardy. Perhaps there's a timeline of sorts, a sense that there will be a resolution or at least some progress to give you hope. But all too often, the uncertainty is prolonged. No end in sight.

Grieving what you are losing or have lost—however painful—is the difficult but essential response to many of these crises. At the same time, some circumstances require us to solve complicated problems and make decisions that have serious consequences.

You are not at your best. Your energy is somewhat diminished and your resilience is compromised. Even if some of your trusted coping strategies are still available, it takes motivation to employ them. You can't avoid feeling vulnerable.

## "It's Not Fair"

At confusing or chaotic times like this, let's start with something basic. This may not be easy, you may not like it, but it's important: you need to dismiss any preoccupation with the issue of fairness. That's where many of us go in our frustration and anger at the bad hand we've been dealt.

It's an old story. When you were a nine-year old first baseman and you tried out for the team and you didn't make it, it wasn't fair. It certainly wasn't fair when you found out your older sister got a bigger allowance than you did. Supremely unfair when the cute guy, the one you had a crush on since seventh grade, invited someone else to the prom.

Other people—well-meaning friends and family—may unwittingly reinforce this issue of unfairness when they learn about your distress. "It's not fair," they declare. "You've taken such good care of yourself/faced so many obstacles/been so kind to others!"

Even well beyond childhood, we may not fully outgrow the implicit assumption that life is supposed to be fair. We work hard, we do our best, and in our mind's equation we should be rewarded.

We deserve compensation for our efforts in some form, whether it is tangible or some measure of immunity from bad things happening to us. It's only fair. Except it isn't, because that's not the way the real world works.

But fairness as an organizing principle for life can have deep roots. For some people, it's integral to their religious beliefs. For others, it has a magical quality—a way to dispel the forces of evil by doing good works and acting honorably. Whether we seek dispensation from a higher power or special treatment from a real-life authority figure, there's a transaction taking place.

Consider, too, that a focus on fairness has a protective function. It's a personal shield against the feelings we would rather not feel. It gives us the illusion of control over our circumstances, to be indignant and even a little righteous. We would rather protest—"It's not fair!"—than face into the fears and endure the emotional pain when things fall apart.

If you're tempted to chant the it's-not-fair mantra, try to give it a rest. Keep your mind open to consider other ways to cope when life unravels, when the doubts and uncertainties take over.

## Reaching Out

It may be immediately obvious or it may take a while to realize that you need some attention from others—to have people know what you are going through. At the outset, you may seek support only from family members or close friends. Over time, the circle may expand to include others, perhaps even virtual strangers. And you will need to discern what kind of help you need. Do you hope, most of all, for expressions of concern or sympathy? Are you seeking advice or guidance? Do you want practical assistance in various ways? Or something else?

Whether asking for help comes naturally to you or the very idea makes you anxious, it's an assertive way to gain a little control when

## WHEN IT ALL FALLS APART

things seem unmanageable. Yes, there's risk involved, the possibility that your request will be ignored or dismissed. More often than not, the chance is worth taking if you go about it deliberately.

The first step is choosing how—and with whom—you want to share your situation. People vary greatly in this regard. Pay attention to what works best for you, on a spectrum ranging from quietly confiding in a very small number of people to posting your news on Facebook. Once you have made that choice, proceed to share your dilemma, your state of mind, your logistical quandary. Whatever is offered in response, try to accept the good intentions even if some fine-tuning is in order. Be prepared with a specific request or two when family members or friends ask, "What can I do for you?" They will be grateful for the guidance.

Unfortunately, it's often the case that someone doesn't get it—doesn't grasp the seriousness of whatever it is you're struggling with. Your crisis may be given slight attention, or met with a kind of well-intentioned but dismissive positivity: "You're so strong, I know you'll be fine." That's another disappointment—a lack of empathy—when you are already shaken by a trauma or feeling overwhelmed by multiple demands. It can feel like a betrayal when that person you counted on, someone who has always been reliable, proves unable to help right now. You may not know, or ever know, the whole story. Perhaps her life has taken a turn for the worse at the same time as yours. Or he has such negative associations to the kind of distress you are suffering—it's too close to home, so to speak—that he just can't respond as you had hoped. Keep in mind that their failure to support you is more about their own issues, not about your worthiness. Try to let it go.

### "Take Care"

It's part of everyday life to end a conversation with "Take care." In this context of things-falling-apart, "taking care" matters more than ever, even when it's a cliché and an unproven remedy for all the problems you're facing.

Think of "taking care" in terms of treating yourself gently. Try to imagine what that would look like, or feel like, or sound like. It may involve forgiving yourself for whatever contribution you think you made to the deteriorating state of affairs—the symptom you overlooked, the too-expensive vacation you wish you hadn't taken. It may mean giving yourself permission to take a nap or turn off your phone for 20 minutes. It may mean an occasional furious outburst in words you seldom use. It may mean allowing yourself to cry—letting go of the fear that once the tears flow, you won't be able to stop. It's not true.

You might look into the ever-expanding market of products and programs designed to soothe the mind and relax the body, even if that's not the sort of thing you normally enjoy. "Self-care" as a concept has long since gone commercial. You can choose from among scented candles, bath salts, foot massagers, meditation videos, and more. What matters is finding some relaxing activity that suits you. Maybe you can rely on something that has been helpful in the past, even if that may be difficult in your present circumstances. Let's say, for example, that your powers of concentration may be diminished, making reading no longer the pleasure it once was—at least for now. Maybe you can adjust, skimming magazine articles rather than tackling that depressing novel your sister-in-law said she knew you would love, the one with so many characters you need a chart to keep track of them.

Or you might try something entirely new as an experiment and give yourself credit for the effort, no matter the outcome. If you've always responded to email promptly ... wait at least a week, unless it's urgent. If you've typically raised your hand at a call for volunteers ... don't. The goal is to give some definition to that well-meant but vague admonition, "Take care." And if your version of the falling-apart world involves taking care of others, recognize

156 WHEN IT ALL FALLS APART

that taking care of yourself matters even more. You simply can't keep giving out unless you rest and refuel along the way.

When the familiar and predictable structure of your life is threatened, it's perfectly normal to be confused by the complexity and overwhelmed by the intensity of your feelings. But try to think in terms of running a marathon rather than a sprint. Obviously, you need to conserve energy for a long race, not expend it all in one burst. That's true of these falling-apart times as well. Try to take it slow and steady, no rushing to solve everything at once.

The way your brain engages with the challenge helps, too. When runners think in five-mile segments or select other markers or milestones along the route, it improves the odds that they can go the distance. When you feel besieged in your real life, the same principle applies. With some effort, you may be able to relieve some of that sense of personal devastation by shifting your focus from the whole to its parts. Try naming all the different issues that are contributing to your distress, from the profound to the trivial. This is counterintuitive—you might think it would make you feel worse, making a long list—but the exercise gives you some traction and allows you to think creatively about specific problems. One at a time.

Even when you feel undone by a cascade of troubling events, even in the midst of crisis, you can make use of your many years' experience at problem-solving. In the past, what has helped you to calm your nerves or boost your courage or brainstorm solutions? Any strategy that served you well, way back when, deserves another chance.

## Gratitude

What's that word, gratitude, doing here? In the midst of a disaster, dealing with a full-on crisis, how can you be grateful for anything?

As you are searching for the answer, try to be very particular. You may know someone who is buoyed by the realization that the sun came up another day, and you wish you had that kind of big-picture attitude. Instead, it's a time to focus on details, on specific aspects of your life that you might take for granted in better times. Think small, think ordinary. The get-well card from an acquaintance you haven't heard from in years. The sandwich maker in the hospital cafeteria who smiled patiently when you couldn't decide what to order. Your phone kept its charge. Your bus arrived on time. By a bedside, the warmth of holding hands. These are moments worthy of notice—and gratitude—when it seems that our world is falling apart.

## Keeping On

It's all well and good, of course, to be so proactive in the face of emotional disturbance and practical uncertainties. But when you are in falling-apart mode, consider a different approach. You can soothe yourself by raising your conscious awareness, not of your troubled state, but of the world around and outside you. Your problems are still there—they aren't going away—but it's time to take a break. In nearly any form, distraction can be restorative.

Have you ever walked out of a movie theater after an engrossing film and felt a bit disoriented by the time of day or the weather or your surroundings? You had been far away from the demands of your personal life, just for a little while. Maybe you identified with one of the characters, maybe you were fascinated by the plot, maybe you just marveled at the cinematography. Whatever held your attention, it was a welcome time-out from reality. That's the kind of escape you need and deserve, even if doesn't last more than two hours. Even if it takes place right where you are, without going far from home.

## 158 WHEN IT ALL FALLS APART

If music delights or comforts you, listen and listen some more. If you have the energy, make a playlist especially for the times you need relief from the pile-on of problems to solve. A quite different kind of sensory experience would be immersion in the kind of listening meditation described previously: get comfortable, close your eyes for a few minutes, and pay close attention to the sounds and smells and subtle movements that come to you in the stillness. If you are more visually inclined, spend time with beautiful objects and images and immerse yourself in anything that pleases the eye. If you live near a museum, make a visit. Or notice the clouds in the sky, the leaves on the sidewalk, the buds on the trees. Or take a few moments to revisit those vacation photos from Mexico you haven't looked at in years. If physical activity has always been your go-to for recreation and—after the effort—relaxation, take a walk. Short, long, slow or brisk, just take a walk.

If you are a social creature, these ideas for solo escape from your troubles may not appeal. You need to reach out to others, not for support—although that matters—but for respite. Enjoy your exchanges with people who know little or nothing about you or your falling-apart world. See what you can learn about them—a sort of late-night TV interview with you as the host. If need be, feign interest in the details. Just leave yourself aside and turn your attention to someone else.

When personal problems multiply, when there's no obvious solution or resolution for many of them, you suffer. The popular phrases may contain some truth—one day at a time, or darkness comes before the dawn, or this too shall pass—but they are seldom sufficient to sustain you. The best you can do is to honor your distress by describing and owning it. The best you can do is to treat yourself gently. The best you can do, sometimes, is to breathe in ... breathe out ... and repeat. Keep on going. Keeping on.

# 19

# THE VIEW FROM HERE

Endings. Stories and plays and films have endings. We follow the plot, occasionally knowing, often guessing, and sometimes having no clue about how the drama will resolve itself—but we know it will end.

So it is with our own lives.

That certainty is fraught with feelings ranging from mild discomfort to outright dread. Or maybe you keep those feelings at bay, opting for denial as your preferred defense against this unwelcome development.

So be it. But let's explore the subject of our own endings. Let's consider the value, both entertaining and profound, of thinking about the lives of those who have gone before us. And then,

## THE VIEW FROM HERE

because our time is drawing closer—at the very least, it's inevitable—let's ponder what matters most to us at this late stage.

Young people seldom read newspaper obituaries, although they may not be able to avoid social media messages. Middle-aged people tend to approach these notices of death with some trepidation or simply skip them. Old people may read the obits with a somewhat different attitude, scanning the names for those of friends or neighbors, checking the age of the departed to see if it's anywhere close to their own.

Some obits and death notices are biographies of people you knew or might have known. Others are simply stories about random characters in the great documentary of Life. Typically, these short pieces have a positive slant. The tributes seldom highlight the flaws or faults of the deceased. Perhaps there's a little innuendo: "She had strongly held opinions" or "He prided himself on his independence." But families are almost inevitably described as loving, spouses as devoted, and friends as close. It's understandable, a wish to idealize the people who leave us behind. It's the best we can do for them, now that it's too late to heal any old wounds. No more time to reconcile our disappointments or resolve our resentments. A fond send-off may be the best we can do.

If the sentiments expressed in writing are genuine—if they pay homage to a life that was truly well lived—hats off to the one who has died and to all who hold him or her in their hearts and minds.

Good obits capture the real character of the life led by the departed, along with some of its flavor. Along with a list of Brenda's impressive achievements, here's a reference to "Barney, her cherished canine companion." We learn that, in addition to his professional accomplishments, "Fred was the two-time winner of the Most Valuable Player Award, Varsity Baseball, Deer Valley High School." And here's Eileen, the avid opera fan, "who was known to participate from her seat from time to time." More details include

THE VIEW FROM HERE    161

where someone lived, sometimes all over the world and sometimes in one hometown from birth to death. Pursuits of every sort are described, from growing prize-winning tomatoes to solving sudoku puzzles, studying archaeology, or playing drums in a garage band. Those who are "left to mourn," as it is often phrased, tell more of the story. Children, grandchildren, wives, husbands, former spouses, special friends—there may be a few entries or a host of them.

The cause of death may be noted. Sometimes there is a mention of the circumstances, such as a sudden accident or a long illness. Or a sentimental description of the ending: "Patti departed this life with her loving husband singing and playing guitar at her side." "On Sunday, April 10, Gene took the key out of the ignition of his tractor for the last time." "At his passing, Henry was surrounded by his family and his devoted caregivers, Mae and Janet."

The obit includes the age of the departed, or you do the math from the dates of birth and death. When you realize that someone your age has died, it's no longer just an interesting pastime, reading about these lives. Recognition dawns that your story will appear in a similar format, one of these days.

Admittedly, this identification with the death of another person—even someone completely unknown to you—represents another assault on your hopes for immortality. Death isn't just for a young person killed in a tragic accident. It isn't just for the 100-year-old lady who received a birthday card from the president a week before she died. The same fate awaits us all.

## Writing Your Own

Make reading the obits a habit. You'll be amused by some of the life stories and saddened, perhaps deeply, by others. You'll find yourself speculating about the newly deceased and wondering if their lives met their expectations and hopes. You'll be intrigued by some accounts and impressed by others. You'll discover odd connections—a person you vaguely remember from long ago or the mention of a place or an institution you once knew well. You'll also get a sense of what you might like to see included in your own obit.

The next step is to think about writing it.

This isn't for everyone. Many people blanch at the very idea. It takes your awareness of your mortality to a new level, not necessarily one you want to face. This concept—that life ends—is made all-too-real. And scary. There's no dishonor in concluding that this is far outside your comfort zone. But if you're having a good day and feeling a bit brave, think of writing your obit as another adventure in embracing your oldness. Besides, you'll get the facts right. And you'll be doing a favor to anyone who loves you and someday reads what you've written.

There's more than one approach to this project. You can write it in the first person, a mini-autobiography—"I was born on March 15, 1951, in Oneonta, New York." Or you can write about yourself in the third person—"Harriet Johnson-Stokes was the daughter of Ruth Johnson and the late James P. Johnson." You can choose the present or past tense.

So if you're up for it, take a deep breath and give it a try.

Start with your name, your nickname if you like it, then record the chronology and geography of your life. Name your family members and the friends you want to honor with inclusion. List your affiliations of all kinds, past and present. Include your pets. Mention the sports you played or the teams you cheered for. Tell how you loved to spend time, your hopes for the world, anything that captures your life and spirit and outlook. You can let your eventual readers know if you want a funeral or celebration of your life and where you would like it to be held. Or you can declare that you prefer to have no such memorial tribute.

THE VIEW FROM HERE    163

Here's part of what my 85-year-old friend Mary has written, opting for the past tense (even though she is very much alive):

> Ms. Reynolds graduated from Sullivan County High School, Class of 1952, and received her B.S. degree in education from Illinois State University in 1956. She enjoyed a long career teaching high school mathematics until her retirement in 2000 and is remembered with affection and gratitude by several generations of students. She was an accomplished watercolorist and a devoted volunteer with the Westbrook Humane Society. Memorial service to be held later this year.

If you do want your loved ones to gather in your name, you'll want to convey some descriptive details about the event itself. It may be too much information to include in your obit, but it's important data to leave behind. If you've created a proper Last Will & Testament, you can devote a paragraph or two to these wishes for your send-off. If that's not your style—or you simply haven't gotten around to facing that task—a letter addressed to those who are apt to make these arrangements will do. You can request that the recipients save your memo to the cloud or keep a hard copy wherever they stash important documents. They don't have to read it now, if the subject makes them uneasy. You will have done your part.

Maybe you want something very traditional. Or you prefer that your family and friends honor your memory by bowling a few frames or holding a big bash of a cocktail party. Maybe you want everyone in attendance to wear your favorite color or tell an endearing—even outrageous—story about you. Perhaps this is the place to remind your family that you want the funeral rites and customs of your religious tradition to be followed—to the letter. Write it all down.

Any plan to mark your departure starts with your own reflections but inevitably involves the desires and concerns of those who

164     THE VIEW FROM HERE

are left behind. They may feel very strongly that "funerals are for the living." They may want an observance that celebrates the life of the departed but represents their own values and—no small matter—suits the convenience of as many people as possible.

Others are determined to carry out their mother's last wishes even if that means hiring a boat and spreading her ashes upon the waters of Lake Michigan on a frigid February afternoon. They are comforted by knowing they have implemented the explicit desires of the person they have known and cherished.

So it makes good sense to write instructions that provide guidance to your survivors, while leaving some decisions up to them. State your wishes. Then add a heartfelt message assuring your family and friends that while these are your *preferences* for a memorial service or a place of interment or a charity to receive contributions in your honor, you trust they'll do right by you.

Let's get back to the obit itself. It's time to write the headline. "Company Founder, Building Contractor," "Mother of Five," "Freelance Journalist," "Legendary Rock Musician," "Immigration Reform Advocate," "Birdwatcher." It's no small feat to select a few words to represent you. Choose something that's genuine. And down the road, if it prompts the curiosity of the random obit reader—someone like you—and inspires them to read on about your life, that's even better.

Keep in mind that reading obits—and writing your own—isn't all about dying. It's also about living fully, which means owning our awareness that we don't go on forever. Add to that realistic attitude a spirit of curiosity about your fellow citizens of this world. You honor their lives simply by reading about them. It's brief, it's fleeting, but it's a memorial. Someday you'll have one, too.

## Paths to Explore

When you think about it, the process of composing your own obit is a matter of taking stock, a life review in a few paragraphs. You

THE VIEW FROM HERE     165

may feel a sense of accomplishment that you've provided these facts of your life, thus far, for succeeding generations—or made explicit your wishes regarding your departure from the planet.

But whether the write-your-own project holds some appeal or not, thinking about closure is only one dimension of aging well. You're still here, living in the present moment. You have the gift of time.

You can use that time to contemplate what's important now. To pose questions for which there are no simple answers. What has been—and what is—the purpose of my life? What if I have to choose between living as long as possible or letting go? What's next—some kind of afterlife—or is this it? This exploration may strike you as premature, unwelcome, even depressing. Instead, recognize it as an opportunity, a time to ponder what has truly mattered—and still matters—in your life.

It's hard to generalize about spiritual concerns and the aging process. Seekers continue to seek and doubters continue to doubt, of course. Since naming things always makes them more real—even in this hard-to-define realm—pause and think about your beliefs or lack thereof. Are you spiritually content or disaffected, secure or struggling? Keep in mind that people who have long ignored or rejected any spiritual aspect to life may move in the opposite direction as they age. A late-in-life quest to make sense of the unknown or unknowable can take them to unfamiliar—some would say holy—places. By contrast, some people of faith turn skeptical as they approach the end of life, especially if they have never questioned or revised their childhood beliefs.

There are paths to explore. If the point is to seek meaning in something that is greater than yourself—be it religious or philosophical or scientific—the key is to keep searching. Maybe you've always wondered if you really fit with the members of some slightly countercultural affinity group that your family looked down upon when you were growing up. Now is the time to investigate, to see if it still appeals. Maybe secular humanism makes the most sense to you. Perhaps you subscribe to a code of ethics that gives you a foundation and secures your place in the universe. If oldness means that a familiar faith grows stronger and its traditions sustain you, stay your course.

There's another intriguing way to think about finding meaning in later life, a pursuit that mobilizes but transcends your own ego. The notion of "Keeper of the Meaning" as a distinctive phase of life is derived from psychiatrist George Vaillant's landmark study of human development. We're probably most familiar with this concept in traditional families. The older generation is endowed with an obligation to preserve the meaning of the family—"this is who we are"—for the younger generation. Grandparents and other elderly relatives uphold what they believe to be their family's values in the face of other influences.

Widening the lens, consider the roles and responsibilities taken by village elders in tribal societies. Through enacting their rituals and telling their stories, they are the keepers of the meaning of their culture for their descendants.

Vaillant suggests that we should go well beyond the boundaries of our own family or community and reach out to the universe at large. He would have us contemplate our late-in-life mission as promoters of such values as honesty, tolerance, justice, and mercy. A lofty thought, yes, but worth reflection.

Think of your most strongly held opinions, the core beliefs that have sustained you throughout your lifetime. Maybe you've done everything possible to assure that this legacy lives on. You were politically active and supported a candidate for election to your school board. You co-hosted an annual exhibition for up-and-coming high school artists. You were deeply involved in your faith community. You wrote letters to the editor of your local newspaper, you blogged, you tweeted. In short, you represented yourself; you expressed what mattered to you and shared it with others.

And if that description doesn't quite fit you, there's still time to promote whatever you care about. It doesn't require as much energy as it seemed to take in your younger days. The emphasis shifts from creation—initiating, inventing, designing, orchestrating—to the conservation or preservation of the things you hold dear.

This endeavor can take many forms, whether your interest in promoting your heritage—your ideals, your traditions—is religious or secular, political or social, academic or artistic. What's important is that you embrace the world in ways that you hope will contribute to the survival (no guarantees here) of what has given you purpose or meaning. Pass it on, pay it forward.

Don't confuse this mission with indignation at the way the world is heading. Keeping the meaning alive is actually an antidote to rigidity and resentment in old age. You're working on your memorial to what has mattered—what you hold dear—in your life. And it speaks to your faith in the future.

During the years when you advanced through childhood, adolescence, and middle age, you had a sense, consciously or unconsciously, that you were moving ahead on life's continuum. As you reach old age, you are faced with the prospect of an ending, whatever that means for you. That's the reality. When you accept that you won't be here forever, you can make your time on the planet matter more.

You can be older—and wiser.

# APPENDIX I
# CREATING A
# PERSONAL TIMELINE

Roger was hesitant to take on this project but found it surprisingly helpful in recalling many details of his personal history. Some events were fairly common or universal; others were unique to him. Of course, he had lived through nearly 70 years of these beginnings, transitions, and endings—but it was a different experience to chart and capture his life story in this way.

First he plotted his age in five-year increments across the bottom of the page or screen until he reached his most recent birthday. Then he selected the categories that seemed most pertinent to his life and added them to the column on the left side.

In addition to the categories you see here, his included "Work," "Relationships," "Health," and a distinctively-Roger category: "Amateur Astronomy." This figure depicts only the first 15 years of his timeline and shows just four of the ten categories he chose.

## 170  APPENDIX I

| more categories | ... | ... | ... | ... |
|---|---|---|---|---|
| activities | playing w/best friend, Susie | piano lessons; safety patrol; Cub Scouts | trumpet lessons; school band; ran for student council and lost | ... |
| education | preschool 1 yr; Maple Grove Kindergarten | Maple Grove Elementary School | Harding Middle School; Franklin County High School | ... |
| geographic location | Westfield, NJ | Westfield, but wkends w/Dad; two summers w/Grandma Cochran in Michigan | Westfield, but Dad moves to NYC w/ Anna; some wkends in NYC | ... |
| family | me: b. 1953; Sam: b. 1955 | parents divorce; mom remarries; stepsister comes to live w/us; Sam's accident, 1959 | Dad's new girlfriend Anna; Grandma Cochran d.1965 | ... |
| ages | 0-5 yrs | 5-10 yrs | 10-15 yrs | more yrs |

# APPENDIX II
# RETIREMENT:
# MAKING IT HAPPEN

Implementing the decision to retire is part practical, part emotional. Here are some suggestions from retirees who looked back and identified what was helpful—or what they wish they had done.

1. Make a plan for how you will spend your time, immediately after your departure from the workplace. What will you do that first Monday morning? The first two or three weeks? Perhaps you'll give yourself some kind of reward for making this change in your working life, even if your financial situation is in transition as well. A trip you always wanted to take, a purchase you've flirted with for a long time, something that represents this accomplishment.
2. Make an outline for your new lifestyle during the first three to six months of not-working. This can be as structured or loose as you like, detailed or not. Of course, you can revise it as you go along.

3. Sign up for something. A group, a class, a club, some sort of activity or program. This assures that you'll be in proximity to other people at some point in your week; enrollment means you're more likely to follow through on your intention.

4. But don't overschedule, fearing that your days will be empty. Now's the time to be selective about your commitments. Remember that you're vulnerable to all kinds of requests made by people who view you as instantly available, now that you're retired.

5. Attend to the various aspects of life that will be altered in retirement. These include health insurance, financial arrangements, perhaps your living situation. Explore your alternatives or options, make decisions—and face the paperwork, one day at a time.

6. Organize the countdown. Edit and delete files as retirement day nears. Gradually take things home that matter to you—books, mementos, the plant that needs more light—and distribute other items to your co-workers. If you work from home, start a similar process with emphasis on reconfiguring, adapting your work environment for the next phase of your life.

7. Practice your response when well-meaning friends or family members ask how it's going. Their instinct is to emphasize the positive—"So exciting, isn't it wonderful, I'm so happy for you!"—when your experience is not so simple or one-sided. Buy some time: "Thanks. It's very interesting, lots of ups and downs. Please ask me again in a few months!"

# APPENDIX III
# TALKING WITH EACH OTHER

*Speak for yourself. Only for yourself.*
Start sentences with "I want ... need ... feel ... " Resist the temptation to represent your partner's thoughts, feelings, wishes or points of view, as in "I think you think ... etc." It's a special challenge, when you have known the other person for a long time. You're convinced you *do* know what they are all about. But your job is to speak for yourself.

*Listen.*
Good communication is a dialogue, not overlapping monologues. Get a rhythm going: *Speak ... pause to listen / Speak ... pause to listen ...*

*Say how you feel, early in the talk.*
"I'm feeling confused/misunderstood/underappreciated/fearful ... " These are the kinds of feelings that precede anger. Express them. Treat them as warning signals, put them into words, and you may get to skip the angry part.

*Limit yourself to the here and now.*
Here's where your long history with a partner comes in. Don't go there, don't reach into the emotional baggage you may be carrying, dredging up examples of past misdeeds. Keep the focus on your most immediate concern.

*One at a time.*
You have your partner's attention. How tempting, to add a few other issues to your conversational agenda, saying "While we're at it ... " That kind of emotional multi-tasking might have been okay when you and your significant other were younger. Now, not so much. Save the next item for another day.

*Keep it in the room.*
Resist the urge to bring in additional troops by declaring how many supporters you have for your point of view. And don't provoke your partner by comparing his/her behavior to that of someone else. There's enough going on, just between the two of you.

*Learn when to stop.*
Try for a balance between too soon and too late. If you're trying to solve a problem, end the conversation when you've reached agreement about a decision to be made or an action to be taken. But if you're talking about deeply emotional issues, you can stop when you feel your message has been heard, or when you have learned something from your partner that requires time to think about. Sometimes you'll agree to disagree: there's no need to pretend you've reached closure on the matter at hand. Take a time-out. Try again, tomorrow.

# BIBLIOGRAPHY

Collins, Billy. *Questions About Angels: Poems*. Pittsburgh: University of Pittsburgh Press, 1999.

Dovey, Ceridwen. "What Old Age is Really Like." *The New Yorker*, October 1, 2015.

Gross, Jane and Krista Tippett. "The Far Shore of Aging." National Public Radio, *On Being* Podcast, May 7, 2015.

Jacoby, Susan. *Never Say Die: The Myth and Marketing of the New Old Age*. New York: Pantheon Books, 2011.

Jenkins, Jo Ann. *Disrupt Aging: A Bold New Path to Living Your Best Life at Every Age*. New York: Hachette Book Group, 2016.

Kinsley, Michael. *Old Age: A Beginner's Guide*. New York: Tim Duggan Books, 2016.

Leland, John. *Happiness Is A Choice You Make: Lessons from a Year among the Oldest Old*. New York: Sarah Crichton Books/Farrar, Straus & Giroux, 2018.

## BIBLIOGRAPHY

Lustbader, Wendy. *Life Gets Better: The Unexpected Pleasures of Growing Older*. New York: Jeremy P. Tarcher/Penguin, 2011.

Lynch, Thomas. *Bodies in Motion and at Rest: On Metaphor and Mortality*. New York: W.W. Norton, 1973.

Oliver, Mary. *New and Selected Poems*. Boston: Beacon Press, 1992.

Palmer, Parker J. *On the Brink of Everything: Grace, Gravity and Getting Old*. Oakland, CA: Berrett-Koehler, 2018.

Sacks, Oliver. *Gratitude*. New York: Alfred A. Knopf, 2015.

Sarton, May. *As We Are Now*. New York: W.W. Norton, 1973.

Sasaki, Fumio. *Goodbye, Things: The New Japanese Minimalism*. New York: W.W. Norton, 2017.

Strom, Max. *There is No App for Happiness: Finding Joy and Meaning in the Digital Age with Mindfulness, Breathwork and Yoga*. New York: Skyhorse, 2016.

Thomas, Dr. Bill. *Second Wind: Navigating the Passage to a Slower, Deeper and More Connected Life*. New York: Simon & Schuster, 2014.

Vaillant, George E. *Aging Well*. New York: Little Brown, 2002.